RUSSIA AND THE RUMANIAN NATIONAL CAUSE

1858-1859

RUSSIA AND THE RUMANIAN NATIONAL CAUSE, 1858-1859

BY

BARBARA JELAVICH

WITH A NEW BIBLIOGRAPHICAL PREFACE

ARCHON BOOKS 1974

Library of Congress Cataloging in Publication Data

Jelavich, Barbara (Brightfield)
    Russia and the Rumanian national cause, 1858-1859.

    Reprint of the 1959 ed. by Indiana University,
Bloomington, which was issued as v. 17 of its Slavic
and East European series; with new introd.
    Bibliography: p.
    1. Romania--History--1821-1859. 2. Russia--Foreign
relations--Romania. 3. Romania--Foreign relations--
Russia. I. Title. II. Series: Indiana. University.
Russian and East European series, v. 17.
DR244.J4 1974   327.47'0498   74-1293
ISBN 0-208-01430-6

For Mark and Peter

PREFACE TO THE REPRINTING

Since the original publication of this book, numerous other studies have appeared on Russian influence in the Danubian Principalities in the nineteenth century and on the Rumanian national movement, many of the latter issued in connection with anniversaries of the double election of Alexander Cuza. Two books cover the same subject as this monograph; these are: E. E. Chertan, Russko-Rumynskie Otnosheniia v 1859–1863 godakh (Kishinev: Izdatel'stvo "Kartia Moldoveniaske," 1968) and V. N. Vinogradov, Rossiia i Ob'edinenie Rumynskikh Kniazhestv (Moscow: Izdatel'stvo Akademii Nauk SSSR, 1961). Two others describe Russian activities earlier in the century: V. Ia. Grosul, Reformy v Dunaiskikh Kniazhestvakh (20–30 gody XIX veka) (Moscow: Izdatel'stvo "Nauka," 1966) and Radu R. N. Florescu, The Struggle against Russia in the Rumanian Principalities, 1821–1854 (Munich: Societas Academica Dacoromana, 1962). A fifth work, V. Ia. Grosul and E. E. Chertan, Rossiia i Formirovanie Rumynskogo Nezavisimogo Gosu-darstva (Moscow: Izdatel'stvo "Nauka," 1969), discusses Russian policy from about the beginning of the century to 1877.

On the question of the events leading to the election of Cuza, three important volumes have been issued under the title Documente privind Unirea Principatelor, under the general editorship of Andrei Oțetea (Editura Academiei R.P.R.); they are: I. Dan Berindei, Eleonora Alexiu, and Trifu Selea, editors, Documente interne, 1854–1857 (1961), II. Dan Berindei, editor, Rapoartele consulatului Austriei din Iași, 1856–1859 (1959), and III. Cornelia Bodea, editor, Corespondență politică, 1855–1859 (1963). Italian docu-ments have been published on this period: Pasquale Buonin-contro, editor, L'Unione dei principati danubiani nei docu-menti diplomatici napoletani (1856–1859) (Naples: Istituto Universitario Orientale, 1972). Letters of Costache Negri, the agent of the Principalities in Constantinople have also appeared: Costache Negri, Scrieri (Bucharest: Editura pentru Literatură, 1966), two volumes.

The general background of the unification movement is covered in Dan Berindei, L'Union des Principautés roumaines (Bucharest: Editions de l'Académie, 1967) and Cornelia Bodea, The Romanians' Struggle for Unification, 1834-1849 (Bucharest: Academy of the Socialist Republic of Romania, 1970). Ştefan Pascu, Marea Adunare Naţională de la Alba Iulia (Cluj: Universitatea 'Babeş-Bolyai,' 1968) should be consulted for the Rumanian national movement through the period of the First World War. An excellent biography of Cuza has appeared: Constantin C. Giurescu, Viaţa şi opera lui Cuza Vodă (Bucharest: Editura Ştiinţi-fică, 1970). Other valuable studies of men discussed in this book are: Vasile Netea, C. A. Rosetti (Bucharest: Editura Ştiinţifică, 1970), G. C. Nicolescu, Viaţa lui V. Alecsandri (Bucharest: Editura pentru Literatură, 1962), and the extensive bibliography Al. Zub, Mihail Kogălniceanu, 1817-1891 (Bucharest: Editura Enciclopedică Română, 1971).

In addition, some of the most interesting material has been presented in articles. A collection of these is: A. Oţetea, N. Adăniloaie, Dan Berindei, Cornelia Bodea, and S. Vianu, editors, Studii privind Unirea Principatelor (Bucharest: Editura Academiei R.P.R., 1960). References to other articles and books on the unification can be found in I. Crăciun, G. Hristodol, M. Ştirban, L. Báthory, G. Iancu, G. Neamţu, and G. Dumitraşcu, Bibliografia istorică a României (Bucharest: Editura Academiei R.S.R., 1970), pp. 172-181; Robert Deutsch, Istoricii şi ştiinţa istorică din România, 1944-1969 (Bucharest: Editura Ştinţifică, 1970), pp. 233-237, and in the excellent study by Dan Berindei, "L'Historiographie roumaine et le problème de l'unité éta-tique," Revue roumaine d'histoire, no. 4, 1970, pp. 745-765.

The author has also published additional material concerning Russia and Rumania in the period. The memoirs of N. K. Giers, whose diplomatic despatches are the basis of this book, have been translated under the title of The Education of a Russian Statesman (Berkeley: University of California Press, 1962, with Charles Jelavich). The narrative only continues to 1847, but it includes a description of Giers' experiences in the Principalities in the 1840s. The letters of Popov, the Russian representative in Jassy at the time of the unification are included in: "Russia and the Double Election of Alexander Cuza, 1858-1859. The Letters of

S. I. Popov to N. K. Giers," <u>Südost-Forschungen</u>, XXIV,
1965, pp. 119-137. Discussions of certain diplomatic aspects of the unification are to be found in "Russia, the Great
Powers and the Recognition of the Double Election of Alexander Cuza," <u>Rumanian Studies</u>, I, 1970, pp. 3-34, and in
"The Ottoman Empire, the Great Powers and the Legislative
and Administrative Union of the Principalities," <u>Rumanian
Studies</u>, II, 1973, pp. 48-83. The first article has the private letters of A. B. Lobanov-Rostovskii, the Russian ambassador in Constantinople, to Giers appended to it; the
second is based on documents from the foreign ministry
archives (Hariciye Arşivi) in Istanbul.

The author would like to thank Paul Michelson for his
great assistance with problems of Rumanian bibliography.

1974   B. J.

PREFACE

February 5, 1959 marked the hundredth anniversary
of the principal event in the formation of the modern Rumanian state—the double election of Alexander Cuza as hospodar of both Wallachia and Moldavia, an act which united the
two Rumanian Principalities under a common executive. The
addition of the remaining national territories of Transylvania
and Bukovina, which were under Habsburg rule, was not
brought about until after the First World War, some sixty
years later. In the accomplishment of Rumanian national
unification and the achievement of independence from Ottoman rule, two foreign powers, France and Russia, played
the chief roles. Of these, the significance of France and the
activities of the French leaders have been studied with great
thoroughness, largely due to the availability of French materials and the opening of the French archives. The Russian
position has long remained a mystery because of the almost
complete lack of documentary sources or specialized studies
of any kind. The following chapters seek to describe and explain, on the basis of unpublished Russian materials, the
Russian policies and motives in the most important year of
the Rumanian national movement and to clarify a major episode in Russian foreign relations in the nineteenth century.
The basis for this study has been the private papers and
official reports of Nikolai Karlovich Giers, who was the
Russian consul-general in Bucharest from 1858 to 1863, the
years of the double election and the subsequent unification
of the administrative and legislative branches of the governments of the two Principalities. Giers' role in Rumanian
affairs is of added interest when it is remembered that he
became the Russian foreign minister in 1882. In dealing
with the governments of southeastern Europe, Russia, as
the other great powers, was concerned not only with the international position of these states, but also with their internal regimes. Giers in his reports, therefore, dealt with
and became intimately concerned with the political

developments in Bucharest and Jassy as well as with the specific international problems. The following study will thus cover both the Rumanian question in its European aspects and the social and political issues in the Principalities as seen through the eyes of the Russian representatives.

The Giers papers relevant to this subject fall into seven categories:

I. 1858. Giers' despatches to Lobanov, the Russian representative in Constantinople, and to Popov, the Russian consul in Jassy.

II. 1859. (1) Giers' despatches to Gorchakov, the Russian foreign minister, and (2) Giers' despatches to Lobanov, Popov and other Russian officials.

III. 1858-1859. The private letters of Popov to Giers.

IV. 1856-1862. The private letters of Gorchakov to Giers and to Giers' wife, Olga, who was the Russian minister's niece.

V. 1858, 1859, 1860. Giers' correspondence with his wife during her summer visits to German spas.

VI. 1859. The private letters of Titov, the Russian representative in Stuttgart, and Balabin, the Russian ambassador in Vienna, to Giers.

VII. 1858-1863. The private letters of Lobanov to Giers.

In addition to the Giers collection, the following material was obtained on microfilm from the Russian Foreign Ministry archives.

I. 1858-1859. The instructions of Gorchakov to Giers.

II. 1858-1859. The instructions of Gorchakov to Lobanov.

III. 1858-1859. The reports of Lobanov dealing with the events in the Principalities.

These documents are designated in the footnotes under the title Russian archives.

The spelling of proper names follows, in general, the language of national origin. Complete consistency has not, however, always been possible or advisable, particularly when a name is well known in another form. I have, for example, used Giers, not Girs, and Jassy, not Iaşi. With the exception of the first chapter all dates have been given in both the old and new style since the majority of the documents of the period are in this form.

I would like to express my deep gratitude to Mr. Serge Giers for his permission to use and to publish the letters of his grandfather. I also wish to thank the Director of the Foreign Ministry Archives of the Soviet Union for the provision of the supplementary material. I am greatly indebted to Professors Warren Ramsey, Nicholas V. Riasanovsky, Raymond J. Sontag, and my father, Myron F. Brightfield, for their suggestions and assistance. Mr. Frederick Kellogg kindly helped me correct the proof. To my husband, Charles Jelavich, I wish to convey my warmest appreciation for the time and effort which he has expended on this manuscript.

CONTENTS

Chapter I

RUSSIA AND THE PRINCIPALITIES, 1829-1858

The signature of the Treaty of Paris in 1856 opened a
new period in Russian internal and external affairs. From
this date until approximately 1877 the Russian government
followed a policy of recueillement—a term originated by its
principal proponent, A. M. Gorchakov. Under this system
the prime attention of the government was directed toward
the solution of the internal problems which the Crimean war
had shown in their true gravity. Hereafter, the great reforms of the 1860s absorbed the strength and energy of the
Russian state. Despite the magnitude of the events between
1856 and 1877, in particular the unification of Germany and
of Italy, and the resultant shift in the power position of Austria and France, Russia remained out of the conflicts of the
continent. In a large measure because of Russian absten-
tion from active interference, the great power realignment
of western and central Europe took place without the un-
leashing of a major war.

The adoption of a policy of recueillement in no sense
meant that Russia avoided all foreign combinations or that
she did not pursue a definite policy. Until 1870, when its
goal was finally achieved, the Russian government in its relations with Europe followed a single consistent policy which
called first and foremost for the abrogation of the Treaty of
Paris, particularly of the clauses neutralizing the Black Sea.
In addition, Russia sought to reestablish her prestige as the
recognized champion of the Orthodox peoples of the Balkans
and to regain southern Bessarabia which had been lost to
Moldavia in 1856.

The Crimean war had also demonstrated to Russia the

mortal danger of isolation. Of her former conservative allies, Austria and Prussia, only the latter had emerged in
Russian eyes with clean hands; Austria was now regarded
as a traitor. Britain remained after the war the constant
Russian adversary in the east and the recognized principal
national enemy. Since Russia desperately needed an ally to
preserve her from the danger of the reformation of a hostile
coalition and to allow her a period of peace for internal reform, only France under Napoleon III offered real advantages for Russian policy. From this strange combination of
Russian autocrat and imperial adventurer came the major
steps in the unification of Italy and Rumania.

Certainly, for the Danubian Principalities the breakup
of the alliance of the three northern courts was the one basic condition for the accomplishment of national unification.
Neither Austria nor Russia prior to the Crimean war had
desired the creation of an independent national state on the
Danube. Both nations looked on this territory as a field of
conquest or a bargaining point should the Ottoman Empire
crumble. Neither of the powers favored the establishment
of national states as such. Russia with the perennial Polish
problem and Austria with her restless national minorities
feared the attraction which such a state might offer to their
own nationals. Moreover, the establishment of a new state
on the Danube would be a real gamble for both powers in international relations. Situated strategically in relation to
both Austria and Russia, and to the Straits, a Rumanian
state would always be the subject of great power conflicts.
Where no clear division of power could be made, it was
recognized that the wiser course would be to maintain the
status quo.

From 1829 to 1856 Russia had been in virtually complete control of the Principalities as a result of the Russo-
Turkish war of 1829 and the Peace of Adrianople. During
this period she had a unique opportunity to establish a firm
base for future prestige and influence. Her candidates,
Mihail Sturdza in Moldavia and Alexandru Ghica, followed
by G. Bibescu, in Wallachia, held the hospodarial posts.
The Russian consuls in Bucharest and Jassy, moreover,
exercised the greatest power in the country. Under Russian
sponsorship a constitution, the Règlement organique, was
adopted which gave the Principalities a more modern administrative system and introduced reforms in almost all

parts of Rumanian political life. Yet despite her undoubted
services to the Rumanian national cause in freeing the
country from direct Ottoman interference and in the establishment of orderly administration, the Russian government
in the period of its protectorate was unable to win the favor
of any significant group within the Principalities. Once direct military rule was withdrawn and the Russian protectorate was replaced by a general guarantee by the European
great powers, the Russian government found that it could
command the services of no Russophil party or leader of
major significance in Rumanian political life. This condition was in sharp contrast to the Russian position in Bulgaria, Serbia and Montenegro, where later Russian political
successes were due in large measure to the existence of
numerous sympathizers within these countries.

The reason for the Russian failure lay not only in the
arbitrary nature of Russian rule under the protectorate, but
also in the social system in the Principalities and the effects of the revolutions of 1848. In her relations with Serbia, Bulgaria and Montenegro in the nineteenth century
Russia had always been able to obtain support from the
Orthodox church and the peasantry, whose members formed
the vast majority of the population. The church in turn influenced the political orientation of the people and was important in national life. When difficulties arose with the
central governments of these states or with the politicians
in office, the Russian government could still be assured of
the existence of a strong underlying current in her favor.
In Rumania, in contrast, Russia failed to win the allegiance
of the peasant, who was Orthodox if not Slavic, and alie-
nated the national clergy in the matter of the Dedicated
Monasteries.[1] Thus deprived of the elements of the population who supported her in other Balkan lands, Russia also
failed to win over the great landowners to whom she gave
her complete backing.

At the commencement of the Russian protectorate in
1829 it was recognized that reforms would have to be made
in the corrupt and disordered governments of the Principalities.[2] Under the able direction of Count P. D. Kiselev, the
governor-general from 1829 to 1834, Russian administration was efficient and enlightened. The material condition
of the country was improved and roads and communications
were developed. The endowment of the Principalities with

parallel institutions was to aid in the eventual achievement of national unification.

In assuming control of the country the Russian government found that it had only one social group with which it could deal—the large boyars. With the waning of direct Ottoman control and, subsequently, with the downfall of the Phanariote regime, this group emerged as the sole power in the government. The great landowner enjoyed a truly privileged position and lived apart from the mass of the people. He paid no taxes and was exempt from military service.[3] He had gained unchallenged political, social and economic supremacy in the countryside although his direct ownership of the land under his control was not established until after the Règlement organique. No other group or individual existed who could balance his power either in the central government or on the land. A middle class in the real sense of the word had not yet come into existence. As one writer expressed it: "The country was but a big estate, administered like an estate—a complex of latifundia in which private law is public law, the inheritance of landed wealth the inheritance of power in the state".[4] Under this system approximately two hundred families in the two Principalities enjoyed a monopoly of political and economic power. Within this group the largest proprietors dominated. It has been estimated that whereas three-fourths of the land held by the boyars was in the hands of these two hundred families, fifteen or twenty of these had direct or indirect control over one-half of the country.[5]

The economic changes taking place at this time in Europe also worked to the advantage of the boyar. After the Treaty of Adrianople the monopoly which the Ottoman Empire held on the trade in grains in the Principalities was lifted. Thereafter, with the increasing demand from the west for food for the growing industrial populations, the price of grains and, consequently, the value of land rose sharply. As land came more into demand, the portions used for meadow and pasture shrank. Cattle raising, which had been the chief occupation of the peasant, suffered. In addition, it was now obviously economically advantageous for the landowner to work the maximum amount of land and to extract the longest hours possible from the peasant. Henceforth the boyar attempted to restrict as severely as possible the amount and quality of the land which he was

required to allot to the peasant and to increase the latter's
hours of service. The boyar also favored legislation which
would prevent the peasant from moving from his village. In
the period under consideration the large proprietors were
successful in attaining their goals. Thus resulted what has
been called "a noteworthy example of how economic prosperity may produce social regress."[6]

The political conditions established under the Russian
protectorate gave the boyar an excellent opportunity to
achieve the type of agrarian regime best suited to his needs.[7]
From this period until the first World War the economic
pattern in the Rumanian lands became increasingly that of
the large estate worked by peasant labor, which after 1864
was in theory free, but in practice servile. The stages in
the establishment of Rumanian national independence were
thus accompanied by a corresponding degradation in the
status of the peasant. Political freedom and national sov-
ereignty, gained under the direction and inspiration of the
liberal landowners and intellectuals, thus brought no material benefits to the majority of the population.

The first major move in the direction of reducing the
position of the peasant was taken under Kiselev's administration. By the political system established to regulate the
government of the Principalities, divans composed of representatives of the great boyars and the higher clergy were
to elect a prince in each province who was to hold office for
life. At the same time commissions were set up to study
the necessary reforms. This system provided an excellent
opportunity for the boyar to improve his position in relation
to the peasant. The most striking change which occurred
was that in the Règlement organique for the first time the
boyar was designated owner of the land. The peasant retained only the right to a collective share in two-thirds of
the estate. Simultaneously, his labor dues were increased
and measures were enacted which made it almost impossible for him to change his residence. The boyar thus in
practice gained both land and labor. The peasant benefited
from the new economic order only in that the many taxes
which the state had formerly collected from him were now
converted into a single tax—a matter which, of course, had
nothing to do with the boyar.[8]

The agrarian measures were not approved by Kiselev.[9]
In a letter to A. P. Butenev, the Russian representative at

Constantinople, he complained that the assembly of boyars, "having constituted itself judge in its own cause, it is only natural that it seeks to extend its own privileges at the expense of the others, who are neither represented nor defended by anyone. That goes so far, that by an insidious clause regarding labor dues they have bound the villagers to the soil, though they are free by right, and every day they tend to make of them slaves, to oppress them the more...."[10] Kiselev's objections were overruled by his own government and he was able to secure only minor changes.

In Russian eyes the Règlement organique was intended to bring prosperity to the Principalities. Whether Russia eventually annexed the lands or merely used them as a military base, it was to her interest that tranquility and order prevail. Certainly, the government of Nicholas I would not rush to the aid of the Moldavian peasant; Russia herself followed a similar pattern of agrarian relationships. Russian patronage of the large boyars was the only expedient policy at that time. In contrast with its relationship with the Slavic peasant in the Balkans, the Russian government found that it had already antagonized the Rumanian peasant.[11] It must be remembered that Rumania had been the battlefield between Turkey and Russia; both armies had attempted to live off the land. The main burden of requisitioning and forced labor had fallen on the local peasant. After 1821 the Turkish troops had been comparatively disciplined; thereafter, it was the troops of the tsar who drew the principal hatred in the countryside.

The additional privileges which the boyar gained in the Règlement should not only have strengthened the only class who could be expected to favor Russian rule, but also have won its gratitude. The landowners as a group, however, never provided a reliable base for Russian influence. The failure of the general policy of backing the large proprietor lay not so much in this condition as in the increasing importance which the western ideals of liberalism and nationalism came to enjoy in the Principalities and the effects of the revolutions of 1848.[12] This course of events would have been difficult for a Russian statesman to have foretold in 1828.

Although many aspects of the Russian protectorate were undoubtedly arbitrary and tyrannical, perhaps the chief weakness of Russian rule was its inability to retain a hold

on the mind or imagination of the younger generation in the
Principalities. The identification of Russia with reaction
and foreign oppression by the educated youth who were to
lead in the future development of the country was a natural
result of the conditions existing in Russia itself during the
period of the Russian protectorate. Russia in the reign of
Nicholas I remained in a state of political and social stagna-
tion in comparison to the nations of western Europe.[13] Education withered; the official ideology of autocracy, Ortho-
doxy and nationalism was applicable only to strictly Russian
conditions and offered no universal appeal. In contrast, the
universities and academic institutions of Europe were not
only technically superior but before 1848 they were the centers for the dissemination of new and revolutionary ideas.
It was to the west, principally to Paris, that the boyars sent
their sons to be educated. Upon returning home this group,
imbued with the ideals of liberalism and nationalism in their
western European context, was to lead the movement for national unification and eventually to exert a large measure of
control in the government of the new Rumanian state.

The Rumanian national movement, led by the sons of
the boyars educated in the west, was primarily a battle of
political concepts carried on through the writings and political activities of a small group of men who adopted intact
western liberalism and nationalism and attempted to apply
them to Rumanian conditions. The movement was thus highly doctrinaire; the liberal ideology was accepted as part of
the process of education and not as a result of practical
need. Like his western counterpart, the Rumanian liberal
called for a political system which guaranteed individual
freedom and for the unification of the people of his nation in
an independent state. Equality before the law, equal taxes
for all classes, equal liability for military service, civil
liberties and constitutional government were all part of his
program. The full implementation of these conditions would,
of course, have undone the political supremacy of the large
landowner in the Principalities.

Rumanian liberalism was part of the general European
movement abhorred by Nicholas I. The liberal group quite
correctly designated Russia, not the Ottoman Empire, as
its real enemy. In foreign affairs Russia through her protectorate of the Principalities could block any attempts at
national unification; in domestic policy the Russian

government was the symbol of reaction.[14]   The Russian role in the suppression of the revolutions of 1848 in central Europe as well as in the Principalities placed the final seal on what was to be a lasting division of interest.   Henceforth, Russia could expect to meet only opposition from what was to become the politically most significant section of the country.   Although the revolt in Moldavia in 1848 was easily suppressed and proved of short duration, the revolutionary leaders were able to set up a provisional government in Wallachia.   Attacking Russia as the chief opponent of Rumanian nationality, they succeeded in coming to an agreement with the Porte.[15]   Russian arms exercised in the Principalities and Russian influence at Constantinople, nonetheless, finally put an end to the movement.   Forced to flee the country, most of the leaders of the Wallachian revolution returned to Paris where, until their return to the Principalities ten years later, they retained the leadership of the Rumanian national movement.

During his brief tenure in power the Rumanian liberal was forced to deal with the agrarian question.[16]   As in other parts of Europe the revolutionary leaders in the beginning called upon the peasant; throughout Wallachia the countryside had been in revolt.   The peasant, however, was not interested in national unity and individual liberties.   He wished to be freed from labor obligations and to acquire a clear title to the land which he worked.   The implications of these demands were too much for the liberal leaders, who were themselves predominantly landowners.   Although they clearly demonstrated their inability to meet or to understand the agrarian problem in 1848, it must not be forgotten that those who favored agrarian reform were in the liberal party[17] in the Principalities.   Throughout the period under discussion the conservative always feared that a liberal advent to power would not only damage his political and social position, but that it would lead to the division of his estates. Although in future years it became clear that the adoption of liberal principles, that is economic liberty, free contract and the sanctity of private property, was really of tremendous advantage to the landowner in this dealings with the peasant, that was not obvious in 1848 or 1859.   At this time a significant minority of the liberal party, of whom perhaps the most noteworthy was C. A. Rosetti, who became the editor of the influential paper, Românul, argued for agrarian reform. The conservative thus fought the liberal for the preservation of his special position in the state, for his political and social supremacy, and for the continuation of the agrarian regime of the Règlement organique.

We have seen how Russia during the period of her protectorate favored and worked with the great boyars, who were the base and strength of the conservative party. Russian intervention in 1849 had preserved them from the disasters of political and social revolution and had maintained their authority in the state. Nevertheless, despite the direct advantages thus gained from Russia, the boyar never became a Russian partisan. With the exception of a few families who remained tied to Russia through family affiliations or service in the Russian government, the conservative boyar, like the liberal, looked westward. Completely separated from the peasant who worked his land, he was cosmopolitan and latinized.[18] Unenthusiastic about the national cause, he preferred to live abroad or in the cities of his own country, in Bucharest in particular. He imported at great expense the articles which surrounded him, his clothes and his furniture. His children were sent abroad for their education. His political ideal remained the preservation of the status quo in which a small group of landowners held absolute social, political and economic power and lived a life entirely apart from the rest of the nation. He did not admire Russia and resented her protectorate. He felt himself a part of the west and Latin civilization.

The boyar justified his special position in the Principalities by his undoubted superiority in education and his administrative experience. In his mind political power was inseparably connected with landed wealth and social prestige. His absolute dominance in his own locality led to his assumption that he should control the central government also. He naturally fought social reform with all his strength. The opposition were designated "reds" and "communists" and were accused of attacking the institution of private property and of undermining the social order.[19] Although united in their political program, the conservative boyars were weak as a party. Their basic difficulty lay in their failure to organize or to accept the leadership of one of their number. Divided into conflicting factions, they failed to preserve a united front at the crucial moments of Rumanian history. We shall see in the following pages how the conservative, despite the majority of seats which he held in the assemblies of the Principalities, was constantly forced to retreat before the liberal party.

From 1848 to 1857 the leadership of the Rumanian national movement remained with the liberals and the center was Paris. There the Golescu and Brătianu brothers and Rosetti retained the leadership of the movement. Gradually the character of their program changed.[20] National unification, not the establishment of a liberal, constitutional government, became their chief aim. By 1856 their program had thus become practical and limited: the unification of Moldavia and Wallachia into a Rumanian state and its headship by a foreign prince.[21] No attempt was to be made to include the Rumanians of Transylvania. The adoption of this clearly defined goal enabled all elements of the liberal group, from extreme left to moderate, to join for the accomplishment of the program. Throughout the Crimean war the liberals continued their campaign and endeavored to build support within the Principalities. Their program remained unchanged through the elections of 1858-1859.

Despite their basic agreement on the national program, the liberal party embraced divergent groups of various social and political affiliation. We have seen how the leadership was taken and held by the sons of the boyars educated in the west. They were joined by the young intellectuals, the members of the small middle class and by an ever increasing group which was composed of lawyers, civil servants, judges and other state officials. The interest of this latter group in the liberal party was not only ideological but also personal. Under the conservative regime, government was destined to be the private preserve of a few great families. Armed with a passable education and the firm conviction in their own destinies these men were eager to displace the old boyar and display their abilities as statesmen.[22] The ranks of the liberals were also swelled by additions from the class of small boyars who, jealous of their stronger neighbors, sought to curb the power of the great boyars. Among these groups in the liberal party there were always many who sympathized with the needs of the peasant. Since support in the countryside was desired by the party, its representatives toured the villages during each electoral campaign. The agrarian question, however, was a matter on which general agreement within the party could not easily be obtained.[2]

Although the Russian government was naturally concerned with the internal structure of the Principalities, it was the international position of the provinces which took precedence in the formulation of Russian policy. From 1829 to 1856, the years of the Russian protectorate, the predominant motives of Russian administration had been to establish orderly and effective governments in the Principalities, which would in turn protect Russian interests in the area. An economically flourishing countryside would offer provisions for Russian armies moving toward Constantinople and stable conservative governments under Russian domination would assure a strategic bastion on the Danube. Russian reliance on the conservative boyar, indeed upon a few families of the great boyars as the legitimate power in the state, corresponded with Nicholas's general support of established institutions throughout Europe. Parallel with the Russian attitude toward the internal structure of the Principalities was the Russian policy of alliance with the great conservative courts, Austria and Prussia, in foreign relations. Together legitimacy and order were in alliance against liberalism and nationalism, the forces of revolution. While this combination existed, the national movement in the Principalities, which was after all under the sponsorship of the left, was faced with immovable opposition.

Although the alliance of Austria and Russia prevented further steps toward the realization of a Rumanian state, it did hinder Russian absorption of the Principalities. Kiselev himself favored an indefinite prolongation of the Russian occupation, which terminated in 1834, and perhaps an eventual annexation. Primarily interested in the preservation of the Silistrian route to Constantinople, he wished to strengthen the Principalities economically and to build up a militia which would be useful to Russia in war. His suggestions were not accepted by the Russian government. Previously, in 1830, the Russian chancellor, Nesselrode, had given the opinion that a protectorate was preferable to annexation or emancipation in relation to the Balkan states because no prior agreement was necessary with Austria.[24] If Russia had attempted to annex the Principalities, she would have been faced with the necessity of compensating Austria since the preservation of that alliance was necessary to Russian policy in Europe and in Poland. The

Crimean war, which terminated the Russian protectorate,
ended the best opportunity which Russia had to include the
territory in her empire.

The Russian defeat in 1856 and the subsequent reversal
of Russian policy under the leadership of the new foreign
minister, A. M. Gorchakov, were therefore of the greatest
significance to the Rumanian national movement.[25] In the
stipulations of the Treaty of Paris Russia was forced to
surrender her protectorate of the Principalities to the joint
guardianship of the powers, southern Bessarabia was lost
to Moldavia and the Black Sea was neutralized. The im-
position of these conditions on Russia led directly to a diplomatic revolution. As has been noted, Russian foreign
policy after the Crimean war was completely dominated by
the goal of regaining the international position held prior to
the war and of breaking the clauses of the Treaty of Paris
directly detrimental to Russia. Not only would a revision
of the treaty be impossible without allies, but Russia could
not afford to remain in a position of diplomatic isolation.
Since Gorchakov deemed a reconstruction of the old conservative alliance inadvisable, the only possible ally remained France. Gorchakov favored an agreement based on
the general premise of Russian support for French policy
in the west in return for French aid to Russia in the east.
The agreement was to be for the purpose of carrying
through what was really an extremely limited policy: Russia wished to change the Treaty of Paris and to protect her
empire during the period when of necessity the principal
emphasis would be placed on internal reform. Russia had
no major foreign aspirations beyond the regaining of what
had been lost in 1856; the resources of the nation were to be
turned inward toward the strengthening of the social and
economic basis of the state. Although no formal agreement
was signed with France and, indeed, no clear definition of
mutual interests was ever arrived at, the Franco-Russian
combination was a recognized diplomatic alignment throughout the period under study.

Agreement with France and the policy of recueillement
signified a reversal of the principles on which Russian policy had previously been conducted.[26] First and foremost,
Russia would no longer be the White Knight of the conservative order. Russian interests, in the direct and limited
sense, not the political shape of a foreign government or its

revolutionary inclinations, would hereafter determine Russian policy. Secondly, since Russia now sought to break the Treaty of Paris, it was obvious that she would not under all conditions support the principle of the sanctity of international guarantees. The issue which emerged in this regard concerned the unification of Italy where the Austrian order rested on the treaty of 1815, which hitherto had been upheld through strong Russian support. Thirdly, Russia now accepted the national ideal in the organization of states, and, most interesting, the plebiscite principle in determining the internal structure of a state. The Treaty of Paris, in a section favored by Russia, called for the holding of elections in the Principalities to decide the type of political organization preferred by the Rumanian people. When the Russian position in Poland at the time is considered, the acceptance of this stipulation in regard to the Principalities was dangerous. Russia was now also supporting a position closer to that held by the Rumanian liberals.

Despite the radical change in the Russian diplomatic alignment, the Russian attitude toward the Principalities themselves did not undergo similar basic alterations. In fact, after the Crimean war the Russian stand in regard to the Principalities was so ambiguous that even the representatives of the friendly powers had difficulty in ascertaining her exact intentions.[27] It was obviously not to the interest of Russia after 1856 to be faced by a united Rumanian state to the south. In Russian eyes the freedom of the Balkan people from Turkish rule was not looked upon with favor when the danger existed that they would form a strong state independent of Russian influence. As long as the Balkan people remained disunited and discontented under the feeble and ineffective Ottoman rule, Russia had a highroad to Constantinople through this land. In 1856 it was quite apparent that a united Rumania under French protection and governed by admirers of the west would not be as easy to handle as two weak Principalities. The open road to the Straits might well close. Russia had not been able to build a Russian party of significance in the Principalities; union would come under the sponsorship of and would contribute to the prestige of the anti-Russian left. Moreover, Russia was too weak for the moment to benefit by a further weakening or a breakup of the Ottoman Empire; it was to her interest to carry on a delaying policy until she was in a position to gain adequate compensation.

Despite the importance of these considerations, Russia supported French patronage of Rumanian nationalism in international diplomacy. It should be emphasized that the Rumanian issue as such occupied a minor position in Russian policy, certainly far below the recognized necessity of gaining an ally. Since France stood strongly behind the unification of Moldavia and Wallachia, whereas Britain and Austria, the Russian adversaries, were firmly entrenched in the opposite camp, the Rumanian question was an obvious point on which Russia could hope to divide France from Britain. From 1856 to 1859 Russia hoped that by firmly associating herself with France the latter would be drawn away from her Crimean ally. In the conferences relating to Rumanian affairs, Russia always backed France, but remained one step behind. The Russian government, therefore, although not favoring the unification of the Principalities, backed the French position because it hoped to win in return advantages for Russian policy elsewhere. In the Principalities the Russian agents were instructed to co-operate closely with their French colleagues. Nevertheless, it will be seen that the Russian government, although still acting in complete harmony with France, openly favored not the cause of union as much as the principle that the Rumanian people should be allowed to express their opinions in free and honest elections. Since these were always conducted under a franchise system which gave the large property owners an overwhelming voice at the polls, Russia did not need to fear the submergence of conservative interests.

Although at the conference of Paris in 1856 the victorious powers had been in complete agreement that the exclusive protectorate formerly held by Russia should be replaced by a collective guarantee of the powers, they were in disagreement on the future political shape of the Principalities. In its initial discussions with Britain, the French government tried to demonstrate that a strong Rumania would be a bulwark against Russia. Although the British government was not convinced, the Russian government took note of the statement. Strongly opposed to union were the Porte, the suzerain power, Austria, who feared the effect of Rumanian unification in Transylvania and Bukovina, and Britain, who preferred to maintain the Ottoman Empire as the block to Russia.[28] Expressing the British view, Palmerston wrote to Clarendon, "The united provinces would be a field for Russian intrigue and not a barrier against Russia."[29] On the French side for the union of Moldavia and Wallachia stood Sardinia, Prussia and Russia. Of the latter three, only Sardinia was truly sympathetic to Rumanian nationalism and her support was undoubtedly colored with the hope that a real controversy over Rumanian union would in some way aid the Italian cause.

As a result of the opposition of Britain, Turkey and Austria, the Treaty of Paris provided that a definite solution of the Rumanian problem would be reached by the powers only after the wishes of the Rumanian people had been expressed. These were to be ascertained through the election of representative bodies, known under the awkward title of divans ad hoc, in Moldavia and Wallachia. The organization of this election proved extremely difficult. In fact, in the next two years the Rumanian question became a major international problem in which the chief opponents were France and Britain. In this controversy Russia, as will be seen, again remained behind France, but still in the background. The issue, which separated Russia's strongest enemies of the Crimean war, played directly into her hands.

The stage for the conflict over Rumanian union encompassed both the Principalities and Constantinople. In the Ottoman capital Thouvenel, the French ambassador, and Stratford, his controversial British rival, struggled over control of the Ottoman government. In the Principalities the Austrian government, in particular through activities of its agent, Gödel de Lannoy, sought to create conditions which would result in a negative vote on the question of union. The Austrian activities were combatted by the French agents, Victor Place in Jassy and Louis Béclard in Bucharest. The two former hospodars, Grigore Ghica and Barbu Ştirbei, once back in the Principalities, showed themselves both partisans of union. When their terms of office expired in July, 1856, the Porte used the opportunity to appoint instead two caimacams (regents), Alexandru Ghica in Wallachia and T. Balş in Moldavia, who were to hold office until a definite arrangement for the government of the Principalities had been made. When Balş died in March, 1857, he was replaced by Nicolae Vogorides.

After a long delay the elections for the divans ad hoc were held on July 28 to 30, 1857. The results, which were clearly obtained by force and fraud, gave a clear victory to the conservative separatists. An immediate crisis followed. France, Prussia, Russia and Sardinia broke relations with the Porte, demanding that the elections be annulled. It now appeared that the French-British combination of the Crimean war had been effectively broken.

In the crisis which followed over the Rumanian elections, Russia stood with France but made it clear that she would undertake no independent action and that she was acting in support of a friend and not because she favored Rumanian unification. The Russian attitude was expressed by Gorchakov on July 26/August 7: "We have been guided by one sentiment: that of supporting France in the steps that she took ... to give the French government a new proof of our confidence and to act as a good comrade to her."[30] Within Rumania the Russian agents were instructed not to interfere in Rumanian internal affairs and to stand for the free expression of the wishes of the people in fair elections.[31] When Russia joined France in protesting against the July elections, Gorchakov made it clear to his agents that unification was not the issue: "Union has nothing in common with the reparation demanded by the four courts. Their collective aim is to assure a free election."[32]

If Gorchakov ever nourished real hopes of detaching France permanently from Britain through the Rumanian question, he was to be disappointed. In a visit held at Osbourne on August 6 Napoleon III and Victoria with the Prince Regent, on the one hand, and the foreign ministers, Walewski and Cowley, on the other, reached an agreement in which in effect France sacrificed Rumanian union for British friendship. In return, Britain agreed to support the French demand that new elections be held. On August 23 before the united pressure of the European powers the Porte annulled the elections of the previous month.

On September 25 Napoleon held another meeting, this time with Alexander II at Stuttgart. Despite Gorchakov's subsequent claims that a complete understanding had been reached, little was accomplished beyond a general agreement that the two powers would coordinate their actions in the Near East and would consult in case of the dissolution of Turkey. The agents of the two powers were to cooperate and France agreed to refrain from backing the activities of the Catholic church in the Ottoman Empire. Again at this interview Gorchakov indicated to Walewski his reservations on the question of the unification of the Principalities, but at the same time he assured the minister that Russia would back any French project.[33]

In September new elections were held in the Principalities. Under the revised electoral regulations the unionists won a clear victory. When the divans convened in October, they voted, as was expected, for union and a foreign prince. The subsequent actions of the assemblies appeared so extreme to the powers that they recommended to the Porte the dissolution of both bodies, an event which took place in January, 1858. With the failure of the divans to reach a decision acceptable to the powers, it became necessary to summon another conference of the guarantor states.

On May 22, 1858 the Conference of Paris opened its sessions.[34] In these meetings France again returned to advocacy of union and a foreign prince. Kiselev, who was now Russian ambassador in Paris, gave strong support.[35] The final agreement, embodied in the Convention of August 19, was the result of a compromise between the positions of France and Austria. The document covered divergent phases of Rumanian national life. Of principal interest are the sections covering the future political structure of the Principalities and Article 46 which provided for social reform.

Under the convention the Principalities were henceforth to be known by the cumbersome title of "The United Principalities of Moldavia and Wallachia" and were to remain under the suzerainty of the sultan and the collective guarantee of the signatory powers. Each Principality was to have separate but parallel institutions—a hospodar, a ministry and an assembly—but a central commission was to meet at Focşani and a single court of appeal was to be set up. The hospodars, who were to be elected for life by the assemblies and invested by the sultan, held the executive power. The legislative power was divided between the assemblies and the central commission. The assemblies were elected every seven years and the ministers were responsible to it. It had control over the budget and taxation.

For all its admirable features, the political sections of the convention suffered from certain obvious faults resulting largely from the circumstance that it represented a compromise between unionist and non-unionist views. Under it a prince desiring to secure the enactment of a measure of interest to both provinces would first have to present it to the central commission, it would then have to be voted by the two chambers, then finally approved by the hospodars. If the assemblies introduced changes, matters could drag on indefinitely. The first year of administration under this system demonstrated clearly the difficulty of its application, particularly under the political conditions existing within the Principalities.

In Article 46, which will be quoted in part because of its subsequent importance, the powers provided certain guarantees of civil rights to the Rumanians and also directed that agrarian reform in the interest of the peasant be undertaken.

> The Moldavians and the Wallachians will be all equally liable to taxation and equally admissible to public service in both Principalities. Their individual liberty will be guaranteed.... All the privileges, exemptions or monopolies which certain classes still enjoy will be abolished, and the revision of the law which regulates the relations of the landlords with the farmers will be undertaken without undue delay with a view to improving the condition of the peasants."[36]

It is interesting to note that in the discussions on social questions the powers did not vote as they had on the question of union. In the previous years Austria had tended to support the interests of the Rumanian peasant, perhaps because the boyars were believed to be in the Russian camp and the liberals with the French. Moreover, since reform had been undertaken in Transylvania after 1848, Austria could safely favor similar measures outside her borders. Britain consistently supported the large landowners and was solely concerned with the political side of the question. Thus on the issue of the necessity of providing for the abolition of feudal obligations in the Principalities, Austria, France and Prussia supported such a provision, whereas Britain, Russia and Sardinia wanted the matter to be handled by the Principalities themselves. The Ottoman Empire wished to decide the question itself without outside interference. Although Article 46 was

included in the convention, the electoral provisions of that
same document, which guaranteed that the control of the
state would remain in the hands of the conservatives, condemned the measures on agrarian reform to oblivion. An
assembly chosen under a highly restrictive franchise could
not be expected to vote away the economic and social advantages of its members.[37]

Thus by August, 1858 a pattern for the future development of the Principalities had finally been set down by the
powers. Although at the congress of 1856 they had agreed
that the wishes of the Rumanian people should be consulted,
they had been unwilling and unable to accept the expressed
wish of the Principalities for union and a foreign prince.
The Convention of August 19, however, gave the Rumanians the opportunity to set up administrations of their own
choice relatively free from foreign pressure. Hereafter,
for all practical purposes Ottoman influence would no
longer be felt. It remained for the future to see what use
would be made of the statute by a people who had hitherto
had little real experience in constitutional government.

For Russia the August convention was as satisfactory
as could be expected. France after 1856 had already taken
the former Russian position as the dominant power in Rumanian internal politics as well as in foreign affairs.
France, however, was cooperating closely with Russia and
both countries continued to send their agents parallel instructions. Both had also agreed to refrain from interference in the party struggles. Russia had also made one
positive gain. Austria was now recognized as the chief opponent of Rumanian nationalism. She in combination with
Turkey had consistently resisted all attempts to unify the
Principalities. Moreover, in Transylvania and Bukovina
she held under her control a large proportion of the Rumanian people. The Russian support of the French position
toward Rumanian unity, no matter what its motives or how
hesitant it had been, was bound to meet with approval in
Bucharest and Jassy.

Notes

1. The question of the Dedicated Monasteries, the
most important single issue in Russo-Rumanian relations,

will be discussed in detail in Chapter VI. By 1859 a large proportion of the landed property in Moldavia and Wallachia was under the control of these institutions, which were administered by Greek superiors and whose funds were sent out of the Principalities for the support of the Holy Places to which they were dedicated. Attempts at reform of these monasteries had been hindered because of the protection which Russia offered them.

2. For Russian administration in the Principalities and the details of the Règlement organique see Jean C. Filitti, Les Principautés roumaines sous l'occupation russe (1828-1834), (Bucharest, 1904).

3. Marcel Emerit, Les paysans roumains depuis le traité d'Andrinople jusqu'à la libération des terres, (Paris, 1937), p. 239.

4. Mihail Eminescu quoted in David Mitrany, The Land and the Peasant in Rumania, (London, 1930), p. 24.

5. Emerit, p. 240.

6. Mitrany, p. 25. For the agrarian conditions in the Principalities see also: Ifor L. Evans, The Agrarian Revolution in Roumania, (Cambridge, 1924), pp. 19-34; and Henry L. Roberts, Rumania: Political Problems of an Agrarian State, (New Haven, 1951), pp. 6-11.

7. Mitrany, p. 27.

8. Ibid., pp. 27-31.

9. Filitti, pp. 66, 153.

10. Mitrany, p. 34.

11. Emerit, pp. 49-51.

12. The sections on Rumanian liberalism are based largely on John C. Campbell, French Influence and the Rise of Roumanian Nationalism: the Generation of 1848: 1830-1857, (unpublished Ph.D. thesis, Harvard, 1940).

13. See Nicholas V. Riasanovsky, Nicholas I and Official Nationality in Russia, 1825-1855, (Berkeley, 1959).

14. Campbell, pp. 46-51.

15. Ibid., pp. 182-183.

16. Ibid., pp. 196-204; Emerit, pp. 303-321.

17. Although the name "Liberal Party" did not appear officially until 1866, the term will be used here for convenience to designate the clearly defined organization of the left. See Constantin I. C. Brătianu, "The National Liberal Party", in Politics and Political Parties in Roumania (London, 1936), pp. 129-137. In the documents of the period the terms "progressives", "nationalists" and "unionists" were applied to the same group. The term "conservative" will be used in the same sense when applied to the right.

18. Emerit, p. 411.

19. Ibid., p. 394.

20. Campbell, pp. 368-369.

21. Ibid., pp. 396-398.

22. Emerit, pp. 367, 408-409.

23. Ibid., pp. 409-410.

24. Filitti, pp. 73, 221-223.

25. The principal work on the diplomatic history of Rumania for this period is T. W. Riker, The Making of Roumania (Oxford, 1931). Of great value also are: F. Charles-Roux, Alexandre II, Gortchakoff et Napoléon III, (Paris, 1913); W. G. East, The Union of Moldavia and Wallachia, 1859 (Cambridge, 1929); Christian Friese, Russland und Preussen vom Krimkrieg bis zum Polnischen Aufstand, (Berlin, 1931); Charles W. Hallberg, Franz Joseph and Napoleon III, 1852-1864, (New York, 1955); Boris Nolde, Die Petersburger Mission Bismarcks, 1859-1862, (Leipzig, 1936); and Ernst Schüle, Russland und Frankreich, 1856-1859 (Königsberg and Berlin, 1935).

26. See Gorchakov's circular of September 2/14, 1857, in D. A. Sturdza, Acte şi documente relative la istoria renascerei României, (Bucharest, 1900-1909), V, pp. 551-554. This collection will hereafter be cited as Acte şi documente.

27. For the Russian attitude toward union see Friese, pp. 144 (fn. 83), 144, 145; N. Iorga, Histoire des relations russo-roumaines, (Jassy, 1917), pp. 321-323; Nolde, pp. 38-39; and Schüle, pp. 78-79.

28. On the attitude of the powers see the works previously cited on diplomatic history and A. D. Xénopol, Histoire des Roumains, (Paris, 1896), II, pp. 547-551.

29. Riker, p. 61, fn. 6.

30. Charles-Roux, p. 184.

31. Extract of a despatch from Bazili to Maltsov, Bucharest, July 5/17, 1857. Acte și documente, V, pp. 140-142.

32. Budberg to Butenev, Vienna, August 9/21, 1857. Ibid., V, p. 491.

33. On the Stuttgart interview see especially East, Appendix Two, pp. 184-189.

34. On the conference see Riker, pp. 158-180 and L. Thouvenel, Trois années de la question d'orient, 1856-1859, d'après les papiers inédits de M. Thouvenel (Paris, 1897), pp. 286-298.

35. Hübner, the Austrian ambassador in Paris, believed, however, that Kiselev personally was convinced that the union of the Principalities was against the wishes and the interests of the Rumanian people. Count Joseph Alexander von Hübner, Neuf ans de souvenirs d'un ambassadeur d'Autriche à Paris sous le Second Empire, (Paris, 1904), II, pp. 182-183.

36. The text of the convention is given in Acte și documente, VII, pp. 306-316.

37. Emerit, pp. 360, 398-400.

Chapter II

THE RUSSIAN FOREIGN MINISTRY AND THE PRINCIPALITIES: GORCHAKOV, GIERS AND POPOV

In their relations with the Russian government in 1858 and 1859 the Danubian Principalities were in a unique position in that the officials principally concerned with the Rumanian problem had close personal connections with the country. The Russian foreign minister, Gorchakov, and the consul-general in Bucharest, Nikolai Karlovich Giers, were related to each other through a Moldavian family; the Russian ambassador in Paris, the most influential post in Europe at this time, was Count Kiselev, the former governor—general of the Principalities. Despite their close association with the country none of these men had any real sympathy with Rumanian nationalism as such. Their attitude toward the question brings into focus the basic contradiction in Russian official policy toward union after the Crimean war.

The Russo-French rapprochement after 1856 had created a strange situation in the Danubian region. It has been shown how Gorchakov's intense animosity toward Austria contributed to his desire to change the basis of Russian policy and how in Rumanian affairs he had not only sided with France but had allowed her to take the lead in questions affecting the Principalities. France, as a result, undertook the former Russian role of the sponsorship of the provinces against the Porte and Austria. But it was not the rule of the conservatives and the Règlement organique that held French sympathies. We have already seen how Rumanian liberalism was French in direction and how strong the personal and ideological ties were between the liberal party and France. It should also be remembered that the liberals

were intensely nationalistic and that their program in its
wide outlines included the incorporation of Transylvania
and Bukovina within a Rumanian state—that is, they envisaged the eventual breakup of the Austrian empire. In
French eyes, this ultimate solution was in no way incom-
patible with the policy they were pursuing in seeking to de-
tach Austria's Italian possessions. France could thus accept with equanimity a Rumania united and liberal.

The situation was entirely the reverse in Russia. Despite the temporary situation created by the Crimean war
and the antagonisms engendered by local conflicts in the
Balkans, the alliance of the three conservative empires had
a real basis for existence. After the Crimean war Nesselrode, when still chancellor and foreign minister, had wisely argued that Russian policy must be "monarchique et anti-
polonaise."[1] Under the circumstances of the time it was
difficult to argue otherwise. Russia could not well support
nationalism in Rumania and pursue a course of imperial
domination in Poland; she could not favor liberal governments in Bucharest and Jassy and suppress far less progressive movements at home. In the internal affairs of the
Principalities Russian interests coincided with those of
Austria and not of France. By staking all her interests on
the attainment of the revocation of the Black Sea clauses
Russia stood in danger of compromising her position in
central Europe and at home. The French alignment ultimately broke on the Polish issue which exposed the weakness of the original entente.

It could perhaps be argued that in this situation Russia
should have followed an opportunistic policy. The threat of
the establishment of a liberal, united Rumania could have
been used as a threat to frighten Austria into acquiescence
to Russian policy in the east; Gorchakov, on becoming foreign minister, could have used the ambitions of Napoleon
III to better advantage to accomplish his own ends. Such a
course of action would have been, however, foreign to
Gorchakov's customary modes of action. In an age of revolutionary nationalism and Realpolitik, Gorchakov was unable to employ the weapons of the new age. Educated under
Alexander I, Gorchakov was proud of his classical education and his familiarity with the world of letters. He
prided himself upon his ability to draw up despatches that
were literary compositions, to play upon words and to

employ classical allusions, tendencies which opened him
to the reproach of having "fait des phrases au lieu des
affaires."[2] He remained essentially a courtier-diplomat, a
"cavalier of the ancien régime."[3]

It is difficult to assess the aims and methods of Gorchakov's policy with any degree of justice because of the almost complete lack of published documentary material from
Russian sources on his period in office.[4] We have neither
letters, notes nor despatches from his pen in sufficient
quantity to study the development of his policy accurately.
From what is available Gorchakov appears indeed worthy
of the criticisms leveled against him. The "Narcissus of
the pen" excelled in issuing instructions which were high in
moral tone and open to divergent interpretations in mean-
ing. He appears also to have been usually one step behind
the event with which he was concerned. Indeed it was his
failure to grasp the specific problems in international diplomacy and to deal with them vigorously and directly that
caused him to rank so far behind his great contemporaries.
In a day when the praise of the public and the laurels of
victory went to men such as Cavour, Bismarck and Napoleon III, who were primarily concerned with the attainment
of definite national goals and to a greater or lesser extent
were successful in reaching them, Gorchakov's reputation
was bound to suffer.

Although in the final accounting Gorchakov's stature as
a diplomat has not been judged high, for he is usually pic-
tured as superficial, weak and vain, without a will or a
definite policy, it must not be forgotten that he faced certain limitations in his conduct of policy. First, unlike
Bismarck, he always had to work in complete subordina-
tion to his sovereign, Alexander II, although it is difficult
to determine to what extend the minister was merely the
tool of his master. Gorchakov himself said that he was
only "the sponge which absorbs into itself the supreme instructions" and also that there were only two people in Russia who knew Russian policy—the tsar who made it and his
minister who carried it out.[5] Whatever the relationship
may have been, it is certain that Gorchakov could not ma-
nipulate the tsar in the manner that Bismarck handled the
kaiser. Secondly, Gorchakov could gain no brilliant victories in diplomacy since Russia had no great foreign
policy goals comparable to those of Germany, Italy or

France. Russian policy was frankly and openly defensive; the concentration remained on internal affairs.

Throughout his career as the leader of Russian policy Gorchakov remained the devoted servant of his ruler and his nation. His attitude was best expressed in a letter which he wrote to Giers in 1863 in connection with a family scandal: "I can do nothing. Now more than ever my family should be Russia. She absorbs all my time and leaves no room for any other concern."[6]

In the face of the contradictory position of Russian policy in regard to the Principalities, Gorchakov and the Russian government solved the problem by simply not meeting it directly. Russia remained tied to France, the partron of national unification and constitutional government, in international diplomacy, but within the Principalities the Russian agents were encouraged to pursue the basic Russian interests, the support of conservatism, the rights of the oecumenical Orthodox church, and the hindrance of further moves toward unification. The implementation of this policy was largely the work of the Russian consul-general in Bucharest who consistently sought to influence the governments of the Principalities towards conservatism and moderation. His actions were always upheld by his government although he often acted on his own initiative in tendering advice.

Another apparent contradiction in Russian policy in the Principalities was soon apparent. Gorchakov's instructions to the Russian representatives in the Principalities had been and were to be along a single line: they should coordinate their actions with their French colleagues and they should not interfere in Rumanian domestic affairs. Despite these clear directions the Russian agents, with the subsequent approval of their government, consistently intervened in the administration of the Principalities. This tendency was to be particularly apparent in 1859 when Giers never hesitated to offer his opinion on the composition of cabinets, administrative appointments and other matters. It should be emphasized that the Russian government in the nineteenth century never adhered to the fiction that the internal affairs of a nation are distinct and separate from its foreign relations. Russian agents throughout the Balkans frankly and freely interfered in the internal affairs of the states to which they were accredited and gave

advice to successive governments on appointments and policies. These practices were followed by all of the interested
western states, principally by Britain and Austria. The
capitals of the small states thus followed the pattern of
Constantinople where the foreign representatives vied by
fair means or foul over the control of the Ottoman government. Moreover, although Russia had been forced to re-
nounce her protectorate over the Principalities in 1856, her
statesmen never lost the sense that they were dealing with
a state that should be, even if it were not, under their wing.

In the year and a half covered by this study the principal Russian diplomatic post in the Principalities was held
by Giers. His role in the events of the time assumes an
added significance in view of the fact that he succeeded
Gorchakov as foreign minister in 1882. The characteris-
tics of his later period, his moderation, balanced judge-
ment and extreme tact, coupled with his relative lack of
warping prejudices or extreme passions, were also shown
in his treatment of the Rumanian question. His despatches
are thus important not only for Rumanian political history,
but also for the light they shed on the initiation of the career of one of the principal statesmen of nineteenth century
Russia.

Giers' early career was completely dominated by service in the Principalities.[7] In 1841 he went to Moldavia as
second dragoman, his first diplomatic post abroad. There
he served under K. E. Kotsebu. At that time Mihail Sturdza was hospodar; by his second marriage Sturdza had a
daughter who married Gorchakov's second son. In Jassy
Giers became acquainted with the leading families of the
country. Among these was that of George Cantacuzino, a
colonel in retirement from the Russian army who owned
numerous estates in Moldavia. He had married a sister of
Gorchakov and had five sons and two daughters. The eldest
daughter married V. E. Kotsebu, a brother of the Russian
consul. The second daughter, Olga, married Giers in
1849 after an acquaintance of three years.

During the revolutions of 1848 Giers became the diplomatic agent attached to General Lüders; in 1849 he was the
first secretary in the Russian embassy in Constantinople.
In 1852 he returned to Jassy as consul. During the Crimean war he was chief of the diplomatic chancellery with
Count Stroganov at Odessa; following the war he was sent

to Alexandria as consul-general. From 1858 to 1863 he returned to the Principalities as consul-general in Bucharest. In 1863 he became minister to Persia.

Giers was thus closely connected with the Principalities both through his family and his early service. In fact, his marriage to Gorchakov's niece was in truth and by popular rumor the basis for his career. Without a personal fortune or good family connections, he was able nevertheless to rise steadily in the foreign service through his wife's uncle's patronage as well as through his real talents and capacity for steady, demanding work. Throughout his early career his wife was not in the least hesitant about subjecting her uncle to a stream of letters requesting better positions. To these Gorchakov answered with patience and understanding. Judging from the letters available he did his best to find suitable posts for Giers. In the first years Olga was satisfied with none of her husband's assignments and generally for quite understandable reasons. Positions in the east were always unpopular in the Russian service; everyone preferred the western capitals, where life conformed to the standards desired by the Russian aristocracy. Existence in the Balkan capitals was rude and often dangerous from the standpoint of health. The maintenance of a household on a western European level was ruinously expensive since most of the items of household furnishing and clothing had to be imported at an enormous cost. By 1859 Giers had four children; a fifth arrived in the spring of 1859. With an ever increasing family Giers' financial position was always precarious.

In his letters to Olga, Gorchakov never ceased to counsel patience and to offer comforting advice. In 1856 in a letter from St. Petersburg he assured Olga that: "Your husband is well regarded here, and will not be forgotten. I will try to help him as much as possible."[8] Two days later Gorchakov wrote again that the best that he could offer was the post in Alexandria and asked if the position would be sufficient for the upkeep of Giers' family.[9] In 1858, instructing Giers to remain at present in Constantinople before proceeding to Bucharest, Gorchakov emphasized his trust: "I have directed the choice of the emperor on you, first, because your talents inspire me with confidence, then and above all, because your character is upright and honest. That last circumstance is and ought to be the strongest lever of our influence in the Principalities, an influence which will be the more solid in that it will have respect as its base. We have not always been sufficiently careful about that."[10]

Despite their close connections with the Principalities neither Giers nor his wife were content with life in Bucharest. In the winter of 1862-1863 Gorchakov wrote Giers a long letter on the alternative positions available. He warned that at present he could only recall Giers, but he could not promise him another post of equal rank. Since Giers had a large family and a limited income, the matter should be carefully considered. Teheran might be open, Gorchakov continued, and "Olga writes me that she would follow you even to Persia." Gorchakov did not approve this move, arguing that Olga did not know what Persia was like. "Do you wish," he asked, "to run all these risks instead of waiting for what I should be able to arrange for you in the future?" Once in Persia Giers would have to remain for several years. Gorchakov concluded his letter by assuring Giers that his position as consul-general in the Principalities was "a post of honor in a time of peril" and that it was more important than a post of minister in a court of the second grade.[11]

Nevertheless, when it was offered, Giers accepted the position in Persia. In 1864 Gorchakov wrote to Giers: "I hope that Olga becomes accustomed to that new life. I did my best to facilitate it for you."[12] Scarcely a year later, after the death of a child from typhus, Giers again requested a transfer. Gorchakov replied that Giers could not leave his post and again warned him that he had no other source of income. He did not approve of a plan that Olga would come to St. Petersburg with the children.[13] Even with this advice, Olga left Persia with her family in 1866; Giers did not return until 1868.

Despite the obvious aid which Giers received from Gorchakov, he either did not appreciate its extent or he hesitated to use it. In the summer of 1859, after he had heard that the post at Athens might become vacant, he wrote to his wife that he did not know how to go about obtaining it, explaining: "I have definitely decided never to ask anything from Gorchakov—and I have no one at Petersburg to prompt him with the idea of sending me to Athens."[14] Later Giers wrote that he expected to receive a grant of money on the occasion of the majority of the heir to the throne. If he did not, he was going to write to Gorchakov "to explain to him my sad position—following the peregrinations that he has made us make since he has been at the ministry."[15]

Although Giers gained much by his relationship to Gorchakov, he also acquired a family for whom it was necessary to succeed or starve. Giers was constantly haunted by the necessity of caring for his large family and of educating his children to a suitable standard. Moreover, Olga proved incapable of handling the limited income available. Giers' letters to his wife immediately prior to and after his assignment to Bucharest contain almost hysterical pleas concerning the amount she was spending. During the year and a half covered here Giers lived in a state of personal tension and anxiety occasioned by a really embarrassing financial situation. He was forced to borrow wherever possible and only with difficulty was he able to gain any amount whatsoever from his wife's properties in Moldavia which were administered erratically by her brother Michel. During the initial portion of his career Giers' first concern was clearly the welfare of his family rather than his personal advancement in his diplomatic career. Although he frequently advised his wife on whom she should seek to know better and in whom she should confide, considerations of service remained secondary. Olga's inability to handle money and her difficulty in keeping servants constantly reduced him to despair. In a typical letter, written on April 4/16, 1858, he pointed out that she had spent 9,000 francs in twenty-five days.

> You never wished to listen to me when I spoke to you of economy and accounts and the like! I swear to you that this year has cost us more than 80,000 francs! —that is to say that if we continue in this manner two or three more years we will not only not have a sou of fortune but even if I am given the allowances of an ambassador I would scarcely have the means to pay our debts.... I beg you then, in the name of all that you hold the most dear in the world, —to change your system completely, —do not think any more of buying the things that you are able to pass by and above all do not address your commissions any more to all the cities of the world for that is what costs us the most.[16]

In 1859 Olga went to German resorts from July to September. The twenty-two letters which Giers wrote in this period are dominated by the same tone of perpetual financial crisis. Moreover, in the first three weeks Giers only received one letter and that from Vienna. Since Olga had left with four small children and a two months old baby, Giers became increasingly worried.[17] In August, in addition to the repeated requests for money which arrived regularly when Olga was away, Giers received a frantic telegram from his wife that her servants had left her, everyone had abandoned her and she was left alone with five children. Since she had addressed the telegram only to "Consul—General Giers, Bucharest", the message made the tour of the consulates before reaching its correct destination.[18]

Despite the constant anxieties connected with his large family, Giers remained throughout his life devoted to his children and he was close to them. His letters to his wife with their dominant theme of economy, nevertheless, expressed throughout his deep affection and devotion. In the summer of 1858 he wrote to Olga: "You reproach me with being dry and laconic in my letters. How little hat reproach is deserved! Who knows better than you how much I adore you and my dear children and how much I suffer from our separation; do not add then, my dear Olga, to my sufferings that of knowing that my feelings for you are not appreciated."[19] In the summer of 1859 he wrote: " ... your absence makes me very sad, — I lead a really miserable existence, I work like a horse and the moments of rest give me no pleasure without you,"[20] and: "May God protect you, my dear ones!— It is my most ardent wish for all my happiness is in you."[21]

Not only did Olga dislike the post in Bucharest, but Giers, despite his past connections, regarded the Principalities only as a step in his career. As we shall see, he was in no way personally involved in the disputes of the country nor did he have violent feelings on the issues which arose. He supported, but with moderation and balance, the conservatives, who were, after all, those most inclined toward Russia. His personal connections with the country were with the section of the boyar class least affected by national passions and the group which stood to lose most heavily by the victory of the national cause. His wife's family owned large estates in Moldavia; part of his small

income came from this source. It would, of course, be
easy to conclude that Giers supported the conservatives because he had a financial stake in their victory and that he
feared the left because of possible agrarian reform. There
is, however, no evidence that his actions were guided primarily by narrow economic motives. He supported the conservatives because their political ideas corresponded with
his; he was convinced that the large landed class was indeed
most fitted and able to govern the state.

The prominence which the Principalities assumed in international relations after the double election of Cuza until
the question was settled in August, 1859 was certainly of
advantage to Giers. As has been noted, the Principalities
did not occupy a major position in Gorchakov's policy or in
his thinking. In the summer of 1859 Giers believed that
this attitude was changing. On July 25/August 6 he wrote
that Gorchakov's last despatches had been very "kind" and
"our affairs here are beginning to attract his serious attention and he agrees with me in all, — let us see to what
that will lead."[22] In August he commented: "Today's cour-
ier brings me still another despatch from Gorchakov who
appears to have decidedly taken an interest in our affairs,
— I am very pleased about it, but, unfortunately, that dou-
bles my work."[23] Later he wrote that he now expected to
be kept in the Principalities for some time "for Gorchakov
begins to take an interest in the affairs of these lands—he
directs despatches to me very often now and always in my
sense."[24]

Giers, however, held no illusions about his position.
"This unhappy post of the Principalities is really a gal-
ley!",[25] he wrote in the summer of 1859. Nor did his opinion change in the next years. On May 24/June 5, 1860 he
wrote to Olga from Moldavia: "I am bored to death in this
detestable Jassy which I loathe from the bottom of my
heart ... My official affairs cause me much worry without
any hope of success; my position is so bad that I regret
every day having accepted the post of Bucharest."[26]

In contrast to Giers' lukewarm attitude toward Rumanian internal questions, the subordinate post of consul in
Jassy was held by an ardent advocate of the Rumanian
cause, Sergei Ivanovich Popov. Moldavia, the "Piedmont
of Rumania", was fortunate in having three friendly consuls,
Place, L. Theremin, the Prussian consul, and Popov, all of

whom were far more enthusiastic toward union than the attitude of their governments or their instructions warranted.
Popov, like Place, was principally sympathetic to the left;
the opposition he designated "Austro-Turks." His general
attitude must have given the impression, at least in Moldavia, that Russia was far more inclined to the national
movement than was the case. Despite their differences in
outlook, Popov and Giers maintained close and friendly relations. Popov complained that Giers' predecessor, K. M.
Bazili, had not kept in touch with him and that he had received his information from Place, who had showed him
whatever the French government sent. Popov declared
himself delighted with Giers' appointment because now he
could hope to return the favor to Place.[27]

It is of interest to note that the French agents in the
Principalities were divided perhaps even more sharply than
Giers and Popov in their appraisal of the political situation
in the Principalities. Louis Béclard, the French representative in Bucharest, stood even further to the right than
did Giers.[28] Like his Russian colleague Béclard soon became linked in marriage to the Principalities when in the
summer of 1859 he married into the Catargiu family.

The pursuance of opposing policies by Russian agents
assigned to the same country was by no means an unusual
event in the Russian foreign service. The Russian diplomat in the Balkans worked under conditions of remarkable
freedom and independence. Individual agents often followed
personal policies in contradiction to the general program
of their government. This circumstance had the great advantage of completely confusing the opposition. The despatches of the Austrian and British representatives tell of
constant intrigues, conspiracies and unexplainable acts on
the part of the Russian agents which were interpreted as
being part of official Russian policy. When these reports
were not pure products of their author's fears and imagination, they were often occasioned by the actions of an individual carrying out a policy of his own choosing. Russian
agents also frequently carried on personal feuds with vigor
and enthusiasm or worked directly against each other in
pursuance of their private interests.

In the Principalities, which had a tradition of corruption in public office, the question of personal honesty was also at issue. On April 12/24, 1860 Gorchakov wrote to Giers:

These Danubian Principalities have been at all times, and with deplorable results, a touchstone for the integrity of our employees. I would consider it an honor to have healed this wound, and my best hope lies in the choice that I made of you.[29]

Although Giers and Popov disagreed on many problems connected with the Principalities, they were on amiable terms. Giers remained in full control of Russian affairs. Popov did not challenge his superior's decisions even though he often succumbed to momentary enthusiasms. Later Giers was to hope for Popov's recall, believing that he did not adequately defend the rights of Russian citizens in Moldavia, but throughout 1858 and 1859 the two consuls remained in constant, friendly communication.

During his period of service in the Principalities Giers was in correspondence with three influential diplomats, Aleksei Borisovich Lobanov-Rostovskii, who succeeded Butenev at Constantinople, Viktor Petrovich Balabin, the ambassador in Vienna, and Vladimir Pavlovich Titov, who with Gorchakov had represented Russia at the Paris conference of 1856 and who was now the Russian representative at Stuttgart. Giers' relations with Lobanov were exceedingly close as is witnessed by the frank and cordial letters which the ambassador wrote to his subordinate. Although the correspondence with Balabin is not as full or as interesting, he did forward Giers' opinions on affairs in the Principalities to other Russian agents, notably to Kiselev. Giers was not as well acquainted with the latter although he made an attempt to see him in Paris in 1858.[30] For Giers' subsequent career, his friendship with Lobanov was most significant.

Notes

1. Lettres et papiers du Chancelier Comte de Nesselrode 1760-1856, edited and annoted by Comte A. de Nesselrode, (Paris, n.d.), XI, p. 115.

2. B. H. Sumner, Russia and the Balkans, 1870-1880, (Oxford, 1937), p. 22.

3. Friese, p. 13.

4. For Gorchakov's career see: Friese, pp. 13-23; Nolde, pp. 23-32; Schüle, pp. 4-11; Sumner, pp. 19-23 and Kurd von Schlözer, Petersburger Briefe, 1858-1862, (Stuttgart and Berlin, 1922), pp. 80, 81, 133, 134, 143.

5. Nolde, p. 24.

6. Gorchakov to Giers, St. Petersburg, January 16/28, 1863.

7. "Memorandum on the Life of N. K. Giers", by Nicholas Giers. At the request of V. N. Lamzdorf, who wished to write a biography of Giers, his son drew up this highly factual, brief account of the steps in Giers' career. This source has been used as the basis for the information on Giers' family presented here.

8. Gorchakov to Olga Giers, private letter, St. Petersburg, April 29/ May 11, 1856.

9. Gorchakov to Giers, private letter, St. Petersburg, May 1/13, 1856.

10. Gorchakov to Giers, private letter, St. Petersburg, May 20/ June 1, 1858.

11. Gorchakov to Giers, private letter, St. Petersburg, December 24/ January 5, 1862/1863.

12. Gorchakov to Giers, private letter, St. Petersburg, February 21/ March 5, 1864.

13. Gorchakov to Giers, private letter, St. Petersburg, April 16/28, 1865.

14. Giers to Olga, private letter, Bucharest, July 27/ August 8, 1859.

15. Giers to Olga, private letter, Bucharest, August 3/15, 1859.

16. Giers to Olga, private letter, (no place given), April 4/16, 1858.

17. Giers to Olga, private letter, Bucharest, July 18/ 30 and July 21/ August 2, 1859.

18. Giers to Olga, private letter, Bucharest, August 4/16, 1859.

19. Giers to Olga, private letter, Buyukdere, June 20/ July 2, 1858.

20. Giers to Olga, private letter, Bucharest, July 14/ 26, 1859.

21. Giers to Olga, private letter, Bucharest, July 22/ August 3, 1859.

22. Giers to Olga, private letter, Bucharest, July 25/ August 6, 1859.

23. Giers to Olga, private letter, Bucharest, August 3/ 15, 1859.

24. Giers to Olga, private letter, Bucharest, August 6/ 18, 1859.

25. Giers to Olga, private letter, Bucharest, July 4/16, 1859.

26. Giers to Olga, private letter, Jassy, May 24/ June 5, 1860.

27. Popov to Giers, private letter, Jassy, October 17/ 29, 1858.

28. Béclard wrote to Thouvenel concerning the August convention: "I see that the immortal principles of 1789, which each interprets in his own manner, serve as the base for the new public law of the 'United Principalities.' ... I fear the introduction, in Moldo-Wallachia, of principles which seem to carry with them all the dangers of liberalism! The Principalities need a strong, honest and inflexible government ... " Thouvenel, Trois années, p. 301. Béclard also commented on Giers: "I like M. de Giers, as I ordinarily like the Russians, who seem all cast in the same mould. Provided with the same amount of amiability, they dispense it in the same manner." Béclard did not have the same opinion about Bazili, but then, "he belongs to the Greek-Russian variety." Ibid., p. 305.

29. Gorchakov to Giers, private letter, confidential, St. Petersburg, April 12/24, 1860.

30. Giers wrote to his wife that he had been unable to have dinner with Kiselev because he had to catch a boat. "If I have given this little account it is to convince you that I have failed in nothing toward the powerful ambassador, who, as I have already told you, has shown toward me much kindness ... Let us be patient then a little, my adorable

Olga, and let us have confidence in the future without wishing to force fortune which is in the hands of God! " Giers to
Olga, private letter, Paris, March 30/ April 11, 1858.

Chapter III

THE DOUBLE ELECTION OF ALEXANDER CUZA AUGUST, 1858 TO FEBRUARY, 1859

With the adoption of the August convention the powers
set the pattern for the future political development of the
Principalities. The next step was to be the election of the
members of the assemblies who would chose the hospodars.
As in those preceding, the elections of 1858-1859 were accompanied by confusion and controversy. Difficulties arose
not only from disagreements over the procedures to follow,
but also over the interpretation of the convention itself.
Bitter personal animosities and a frantic struggle for position among the leaders clouded the campaign conducted by
the opposing parties.

The instructions on how to meet the new situation
which Gorchakov sent to his agents were largely negative in
nature.[1] Although restating Russian sympathies with the
Balkan Orthodox Christians, Gorchakov disclaimed any
Russian aims or particular interests. Russia did not herself seek exclusive control in the Principalities, but she
would under no circumstances tolerate the predominance of
another power. Ideally Russia wished the maintenance of a
neutral area under the protection of the guarantees given by
the great powers.

On the question of Rumanian interests alone, Russia desired that the Principalities retain the rights which they
had received and continue to progress in the future. In this
respect Russian traditional policy remained unaltered, but
the means by which her aims could be obtained had now
changed. The substitution of the collective guarantee of the
Principalities by the great powers for the former sole
sponsorship by Russia, which had been one of the major

results of the Crimean war, signified that where hitherto
Russia had worked alone in defending Rumanian interests
against the Porte, she could now expect the support of Europe. If obstacles were encountered, others would help.
Russian policy was to be:

> Thus, as long as the state of affairs created
> by the last war continues, our mission in the
> Principalities as throughout the east, will be to
> make sure that the agreements which have brought
> about this condition are respected, because they
> dedicate to the profit of the Christian peoples the
> fruits of our persevering efforts, even though they
> stem from a way of thinking hostile to us, because
> they raise a barrier to serious complications, be-
> cause their maintenance is the only pledge of
> peace, and because in order to be observed by
> those whose inclinations they obstruct, they must
> be respected by those whose interests and security
> they protect.

From this policy arose two problems. In the first
place, the Porte and the powers who supported her had to
be prevented from infringing on the terms of the August
convention. The Russian representatives were to watch
carefully that the Porte did not accomplish this purpose by
arbitrarily interpreting the terms of the new organic statute
or by interfering in the elections, the discussions of the
assemblies and the activities of the two administrations.

In their relations with the Rumanian people the Russian
agents were advised "to enlighten public opinion and the influential men in the two Principalities on their true interests." It should be emphasized that although the convention
might be imperfect it was nevertheless the basis of political life and the Rumanian leaders should work within its
framework. In other words, the Rumanians should be advised to perfect the organization that they had been given
and not seek further steps toward union. It would be difficult enough to implement the August convention. Passions
would be awakened; "ambitions excited; hostile political influences will be set to work in order to exploit these seeds
of discord; they will find a propitious occasion in the agitations of public feeling at the time of the elections of the assemblies and those of the hospodars." These disorders
might in turn provoke international complications and compromise the future of the country. The task of the

administration of the Principalities was to disprove the
charge that "their national and independent administration
was not compatible with the existence of the Ottoman Empire."

In the controversies in Rumanian politics the Russian
agents were to remain neutral, but:

> Our role should not at all be sterile and pas-
> sive. But its activity should rest outside of all in-
> trigue. Our influence should not be based on like
> means. The consul of Russia, without coming to
> terms with any party, should acquire the authority
> necessary to make his salutary counsels heard by
> the rectitude of his conduct, by the respect and
> confidence that it wins him.
> The Imperial Cabinet does not favor anyone;
> it has neither candidates to produce nor individu-
> als to protect. It even abstains from relying on
> the past.

The principal adversary of Russia in the task of maintaining a firm government in the Principalities on the basis
of the previous treaties was Austria, whose activities took:

> ... every form and admit every means. She has
> laid the foundations of her domination over the
> Principalities by a political, industrial and com-
> mercial assimilation towards which the Cabinet of
> Vienna works without respite. Political influence
> on those who hold power, mysterious action on the
> parties, an appeal to passions, an abusive exten-
> sion of consular jurisdiction, intervention in all
> the financial, commercial and industrial affairs of
> the country, administrative and even territorial
> infringements—every means is acceptable to her.
> This pernicious activity is particularly hostile
> to us. It requires a diligent surveillance on your
> part.

Britain, although now following Austria and the Porte,
was not acting consistently or in conformity "to her principles, to her liberal traditions and to the conditions of a
popularity which she has always sought."

In support of her policies, Russia expected aid from
Prussia and France. The former, although with no direct
interests involved, would support Russian policy and the
Russian agents could expect cooperation from their Prussian colleagues. France, as a result of the entente

established at Stuttgart, which was based primarily on agreement on the eastern question, was, however, the power whose interests lay closest to those of Russia. The Russian representatives were directed to work with and to support their French counterparts.

The instructions of Gorchakov to Giers and Popov were thus to maintain strictly the order established in August. They were to seek the regular development of Rumanian institutions and to prevent infringements on Rumanian rights by the Porte and Austria. In a negative sense they advised against further steps toward union and were extremely precise in their warnings against further disorders. In general, this document was typical of Gorchakov; the entire despatch is lengthy, verbose and full of fine moral sentiments. In practice, it could cover almost any possible policy which a local agent might wish to pursue. It will be seen how Giers and Popov each emphasized a different portion of the instructions and ended in opposite camps. Popov, the zealous advocate of Rumanian nationalism, based his actions on the sections which emphasized the blocking of Austrian and Turkish activity. Giers, in contrast, preferred to seek the maintenance of order and the status quo in Rumanian political, economic and social life.

When the decisions of the Conference of Paris reached Jassy, Popov greeted the results with favor:

> ... I believe that it [the convention] could not better serve our interests and this is why. The electoral law based on income, that is to say, on all that is most variable and most difficult to establish even in better organized countries; the senate-Focşani or central committee as it is called here, which will necessarily be divided into two enemy camps or entirely hostile to the hospodars; this all seems likely to produce a number of small complications which will provide opportunities for intervention for the guarantor powers and will thus provoke friction between the westerners which will be to our advantage; provided, however, that this friction does not endanger the peace before the proper moment! Let us prepare ourselves to see serious disorders on the occasion of the elections.[2]

Writing later he reported the unhappy impression made upon the Wallachians by the August convention.

The effect that it has produced here is not
very satisfactory; no one I know is satisfied with
it: neither the friends of the old system nor the so-
called progressives; the one group because it had
counted on a more liberal constitution, the other
because privileges have been abolished.[3]

On the work of the conference of the powers, Popov
commented: "I believe that the result is slight, and that it
could have been obtained with less difficulty."[4]

The convention provided that in the period before the
elections the government of the Principalities should be
carried on by a special caimacamie (Regency) consisting in
each province of the three ministers of the last reigning
hospodar.[5] In Moldavia the positions were thus taken by
A. Panu, V. Sturdza and S. Catargiu. Of these Panu and
Sturdza were unionists and Catargiu a conservative. Thus
in Moldavia the liberals dominated and the conservatives
were in a minority, a situation which was particularly disliked by Austria and the Porte who feared further steps toward union in the Principalities. In Wallachia exactly the
opposite condition prevailed. The ultra-conservatives, I.
Manu and E. Băleanu, held the majority against their moderate conservative colleague, I. A. Filipescu. In the ensu-
ing controversies Popov, as could be expected, sided with
the liberal majority in Moldavia; Giers, on the other hand,
did not support Popov's partisan stand in Jassy and in Bucharest he preferred the moderate position of Filipescu.

Unfortunately, not only were the caimacamies split,
but it was not clear either to the consuls or to the caimacamies themselves exactly what their powers were or what
should be done in case of a disagreement between the three
It was not even known if unanimous agreement was necessary for action or if a majority vote was sufficient. As
both caimacamies were divided two to one, this was a grav
problem, particularly since decisions of major importance
for the future of the Principalities had to be reached. In
the first place, the appointments which had to be made to
administrative positions were vital for both parties. Each
faction and each candidate for the hospodarship naturally
wished to place its men in strategic positions. In the second place, the caimacamies had to supervise the drawing
up of the election lists and conduct the elections. Since
corruption and illegality had characterized previous

elections, it was recognized that the party in power at the time would have a great advantage at the polls. It was on these two issues that the caimacamies fell apart.

In Moldavia the formation of the caimacamies was a blow to the hopes of Vogorides, who was now displaced from his previous position. During his period in office he had carefully filled the administration with his own partisans. Since the stipulations of the convention resulted in the return to power of his political opponents, who had served under G. Ghica, the administration of the province was in a turmoil. Instead of a united concentration on the elections at hand and on the establishment of a stable government which could best utilize the institutions bestowed on the country by the powers, the parties and their leaders immediately entered into an intense struggle for power. At first, the three caimacams were united in their determination to make a clean sweep of the Vogorides appointees, but they soon fell out among themselves on who should fill the vacancies created. Catargiu, the conservative, had aspirations for himself for the hospodarship and soon quarreled with his unionist colleagues. When the three caimacams took again the portfolios they had formerly held, Catargiu, who had been minister of interior under Ghica, gained an advantage which he immediately sought to exploit.[6] In the conflict which followed, Catargiu finally withdrew from the meetings of the group. Panu and Sturdza thereupon took the matter of appointments into their own hands, invoking the right of majority rule. In reply to these actions, Catargiu appealed to the Porte through its commissioner, Afif Bey. Remonstrances were addressed to the two caimacams covering not only the question of the wholesale discharge of employees, but also that of the Dedicated Monasteries and the new decree granting freedom to the press. Panu and Sturdza in answer expelled Afif Bey and recalled the Moldavian agent, Fotiades, from his post in Constantinople. The resultant complications, which involved the great powers, were not settled satisfactorily and were finally simply forgotten after the elections when new problems were brought to the fore.

In the controversy between the caimacams, the subject which dominated Moldavian political life until after the elections, Popov at first remained aside. On October 30/November 11 he wrote to Giers:

> I have adopted in conformance with the min-
> isterial instructions an attitude of <u>benevolent</u> im-
> <u>partiality</u>. I say, if necessary, frankly what I
> think, but I do not seek occasions to do so. Let us
> still for some time let others take the lead in the
> affairs of these lands: let them have all of the re-
> sponsibility. Freedom was just granted to the
> press. Now we are going to see all of the disor-
> ders of the parties come to light.[7]

Two weeks later when it appeared that Catargiu had
sought the support of Austria and the Porte, Popov abandoned any attempt at impartiality in the struggle between
the caimacams. An attempt had been made at a reconciliation on the basis that Catargiu would recognize the legality
of the nominations made by his colleagues during the time
when he did not take part in their deliberations. In return,
Panu and Sturdza were to change some of their appointments in the ministry of interior to conform to the wishes
of Catargiu. At first, Catargiu had been willing to discuss
the matter, but, afterwards, "yielding to the suggestions of
Turkey and of Austria he refused flatly."[8] In discussing the
matter with Popov, Catargiu said that he preferred "a decision from above to a reconciliation which in any case
could not be durable, that he had complained to Constantinople and that he would wait."[9]

As a result of Catargiu's appeal to the Porte, Popov
now gave his entire support to Sturdza and Panu and strongly denounced Catargiu's influence. In his letters to Giers
he argued that it was necessary for the two caimacams to
act alone and that their decisions would be legal despite
Catargiu's withdrawal. The caimacamie had to prepare for
the elections within a time limit; they could not remain idle:

> I agree that we should avoid complications
> but if the Turco-Austrians want them in general—
> and that is clear—what can be done! It is neces-
> sary to accept the situation on a day to day basis.
> In the meantime, let us try to make their intrigues
> distasteful to them by the firmness of our attitude
> and the integrity of our principles.... Here, Sturd-
> za and Panu, whatever their moral principles are,
> whatever their personal interests may be (and that is
> another question), are as it happens at this moment
> the defenders of autonomy and the national cause...
> The two caimacams are unassailable <u>where</u> <u>their</u>

right to proceed jointly is concerned as long as
their colleague remains voluntarily isolated.[10]

Popov continued that he believed that it was the Russian
role to preach accord and agreement, and this he had always done. He appealed, in conclusion, to Giers to support
his championship of the two caimacams.

Unlike Popov Giers was not enthusiastic about the positions taken by Sturdza and Panu. He greatly regretted the
incident since it made a regular development of affairs in
Moldavia impossible and confused the question of the application of the convention. He believed that the caimacams
had acted illegally and that Catargiu had been driven into
the attitude which he had taken by the actions of his colleagues. Giers especially condemned the mass dismissals
which were not justified by the August convention or by the
previous statutes regulating the administration of the Principalities. He feared that such actions would drive the opposing party into the arms of Turkey or Austria and that it
would be the fault of the caimacams. He also believed that
their attitude toward Afif Bey had been wrong and that it
could lead to unfortunate complications. Béclard, Giers
reported, shared these opinions on the Moldavian caimacamie. Again Popov was advised to recommend conciliation and to point out to the caimacams the limits of their
powers. Béclard was going to send similar instructions to
Place.[11]

The position adopted by Giers was that generally accepted by the powers. A conference of ambassadors was
held in Constantinople on November 15/27 at the British
embassy to discuss the actions of the two Moldavian caimacams. As a result of the meeting, the latter received a
reprimand on their attitude toward the Turkish commissioner and their handling of the question of appointments
and dismissals. Although some matters might be settled
by majority vote, issues involving the interpretation of the
convention or the firmans were to be referred to the Porte.[12]
When this decision together with several messages from
the suzerain power failed to impress Sturdza or Panu, the
Porte indicated that the elections might be suspended. The
danger also existed that the Porte might refuse to recognize
the results of the Moldavian elections held under these circumstances.

Despite the decisions of the powers and the attitude of his superior, Popov, apparently in concert with Place and Theremin, continued to take an active personal interest in the elections and he made no attempt to cover his personal inclinations.[13] His particular villain had now become the former hospodar Mihail Sturdza, one of the principal candidates for the Moldavian hospodarship. Of him Popov wrote the following:

> He is the true man of Turkey and Austria; and has brought 300 thousand ducats to have himself elected. All the fine formulas, all the principles proclaimed by the Treaty of Paris and the convention, the preoccupations of the powers, the labors of diplomacy to reorganize the Principalities—that all that should result in the old system of demoralization, without the Russian protectorate, —that all that should be reduced to nothing before sacks of money! I am not at all of the opinion that it suits us to work precisely against the candidature of that old sorcerer, but to patronize him, that would be absolutely contrary to the principles that we profess. To decide in favor of Catargiu in the present circumstances is to favor Mihail Sturdaz.[14]

Popov further reported that the efforts made by himself, Place and Theremin, assisted by the British consul, H. Churchill, to sonciliate the caimacamie would probably not succeed because "the Austro-Turk aim is to maintain discord.... In contributing to wound the pride of the progressive party and in aiding in the triumph of the Austro-Turks, we will lose our moral credit."[15]

On November 29/December 11 Popov complained that Gödel, Afif and M. Sturdza had formed a "real camp" and were laying siege to the caimacamie. "As for me, I can only continue to plead their cause. I cannot act at once against my convictions based on an examination of the facts and ultimately against our interests such as I understand them and such as they are defined in the ministerial instructions." The latter had told the Russian agents to uncover all Austro-Turk manoeuvres and "these are developing in full daylight."[16] Two weeks later he wrote an even more impassioned plea, arguing that Russia should neither favor nor combat M. Sturdza: "But that is not the question. It is a question for us to know if it suits us or not to strike our colors before Austria by abandoning our role as defenders of right, autonomy and nationality."[17] In a report of December 27/ January 8 Popov declared himself for P. Mavrogheni, one of the prominent candidates of the left, for hospodar. Although he was "incontestably the best", Popov did not believe that his choice would win.[18]

Although the Wallachian caimacamie functioned more smoothly than its counterpart in Moldavia, a conflict, nevertheless, arose over the question of the interpretation of the electoral law. The August convention had provided for a highly restricted franchise. Only those with a minimum income of 1,000 ducats in land or an urban commercial income of 6,000 ducats participated in direct elections. They chose two deputies for each district. A second class, which included those with an income of 100 ducats, voted for three electors in each district, who in turn chose a single representative. The assemblies were thus to be left safely in the hands of the large landowners.[19] In both Moldavia and Wallachia, however, controversies arose over the composition of the electoral lists drawn up under these regulations.

In Moldavia the caimacamie under the control of the liberals immediately attempted to interpret the regulations in such a manner that the number voting in direct elections would be increased beyond that originally intended. Giers, when he heard of this, declared himself absolutely opposed to any such action. On November 21/ December 3 he directed Popov immediately to protest.

> Meanwhile, in view of the importance which this question, which is connected with the political tendencies of a neighboring country, has for us, I do not hesitate, sir, to engage you to provoke an explanation from the caimacams on this subject and to make them appreciate all the irregularity of a measure which threatens to introduce into future elective assemblies of Moldavia elements which, in the opinion of the powers signatory to the convention, cannot be admitted.[20]

In a despatch to Butenev Giers wrote that the measure would have a "great effect on the composition of the future Moldavian assembly in having enter into it elements which would not possess the necessary guarantees of order and stability."[21] Before the elections were held Giers had the satisfaction of seeing the regulations altered to his approval.

In Wallachia the conflict arose over the attempt of the caimacamie not to extend the franchise, as had been the case in Moldavia, but instead to give a highly restrictive interpretation to the electoral laws. When the courts refused to uphold their views on the matter, the two ultra-conservative caimacams, Manu and Băleanu, attempted to annul the decisions of the tribunals. In doing this they came into conflict with their colleague, Filipescu, the minister of justice, whom Giers admired and supported. In the controversy which followed, which involved the consuls of the powers and the Porte, the two caimacams were eventually forced to surrender, although they did not fully comply until it was too late for their instructions to reach the outlying districts before the voting began. In this question Giers took a strong stand behind the moderate position of Filipescu.[22] Giers deeply regretted the actions of Manu and Băleanu, who were acting in the interest of those who supported Ştirbei and Bibescu. Although Giers believed that the failure of either of these two candidates to win the coveted position was not to be regretted, nevertheless: "it is to be feared that the resentment so keenly excited against these two ex-hospodars will reflect at the same time on all of the conservatives of whom a great number gave their support to the violent measures of the caimacamie."[23]

The election proceedings in both Moldavia and Wallachia had thus to a degree been compromised. In his final despatch before the elections Giers went out of his way to emphasize to his government that the previous violations of the convention had been corrected to an extent that no reason now existed why the elections should not be held.[24] In a letter to Balabin Giers commented that the assemblies, once chosen, would be able to deal with any illegalities that had occurred during the time of the verification of credentials. The only danger that could arise would be should the infractions of the regulations be so numerous that the majority of the assembly would be composed of those elected under dubious circumstances, which would necessitate the annulment of the elections, a possibility that Giers admitted "makes me shudder" since it would involve another period of uncertainty.[25]

The attitude of Giers in support of the necessity of

proceeding as planned with the elections paralleled the position taken at Constantinople by Lobanov with the approval of Gorchakov. Despite the fact that it was obvious that illegalities had occurred in both Principalities and that it was to be regretted that the caimacamies had failed to cooperate to adopt identical electoral regulations for both provinces, Lobanov, nevertheless, argued strongly against the desire expressed by the Porte to postpone the elections or to take action against the caimacams.[26] He was also not enthusiatic about the suggestion that a conference of powers be called to deal with the matter. Again the British and Austrian agents at Constantinople, Bulwer and Prokesch, stood behind the Ottoman demands.[27] In contrast, France, Russia and Prussia favored the holding of the elections and the recognition of their results.

The chief objection of the Porte centered on the electoral proceedings in Moldavia where it was justly feared that the national party would dominate the assembly, It should be again emphasized that the Russian desire that the elections be held on schedule in no way signified a desire to aid the cause of Rumanian nationalism. Two days before the election of Cuza in Jassy, Lobanov wrote to Gorchakov:

> Our consul-general in the Danubian Principalities just sent me the very serious information that, according to what our consul in Jassy reports, the idea of asking for union with a foreign prince makes great progress in Moldavia among the deputies of all the parties. If the Moldavian assembly expressed a wish so little in accord with the Convention of August 7/19, it would be a victory for the Porte, which is only too disposed to declare it [the assembly] illegal, and I can only associate myself with the advice that M. de Giers informs me that he has recommended to M. Popov—that of observing an extreme prudence in order not to give encouragement to such a project.

To this judgment the tsar added the marginal comment, "Bien fait."[28]

Elections were held first in Moldavia in the last week in December. Although Moldavia offered the best hope for the liberals, they gained only about half of the sixty-four seats. Their opposition, however, was split because of the rival candidacies of M. Sturdza and his son Grigore.[29] By caucusing beforehand and standing united behind their candidate, the liberals succeeded in obtaining the election of one of their number, Alexandru Ioan Cuza, who was formally chosen by the Moldavian assembly on January 5/17.[30]

True to his instructions Popov had openly supported no candidate. Although sympathetic to the left in Moldavian politics, he was at first reserved in his attitude toward Cuza, with whom he was not personally acquainted. Four days after the election he wrote to Giers: "We will watch his conduct; if it does not suit us we will attack him, and we will be able to do it freely for the simple reason that we have not patronized the individual." Popov approved of the results of the election and pointed out that Russia had achieved a favorable outcome while remaining faithful to the principle of disinterestedness. He fully expected Cuza to be confirmed and requested authorization to announce the Russian consent to his choice before the prince was invested. The action would make an excellent impression and would help Popov's relations with the hospodar.[31]

By January 16/28, a week later, Popov had become completely captivated by Cuza and wrote: "If the Wallachians succeed in electing a man like Cuza, what a defeat for the Austrians! I confess to you that the new prince has conquered me, and my relations with him will be, I hope, very pleasant: he is a very frank man, very straightforward, going right to the point; with that a caustic wit and shrewdness...." Popov also reported that some of the aristocracy did not like Cuza, whose household was simple and bourgeois; they accused Place and Popov of having "worked for the ruin of the Moldavian aristocracy." Again Popov pleaded for permission "to say to him some petites douceurs" on the part of the Russian government. He concluded with: "As for my personal attitude, it already has a very pronounced character; I am for Cuza frankly and openly even at the risk of compromising myself if, by chance, he is not recognized."[32]

In both of the preceding letters Popov discussed the possibility of a double election of Cuza, but he assured Giers that the prince was involved in no intrigues. In fact, Cuza had sent a "person of confidence" to Popov to assure him that if those who wished to involve him in this direction moved, "he would shut them up in jail." In the second letter he reported more fully on an apparent conspiracy of G. Sturdza, who had evidently advised Cuza to act to have

himself proclaimed prince in both provinces. Sturdza favored the assembling of a corps of volunteers at Focşani to
invade Wallachia. Popov hoped that Cuza's firm attitude toward this proposal would recommend him to the powers.[33]
Popov's strong espousal of Cuza was echoed in Giers' despatches, which also argued for the prince's recognition and
emphasized that the election had followed the rules.[34]

Attention next shifted to Wallachia where elections
were scheduled to be held on January 20/ February 1 to
January 22/ February 3. Although Giers in his despatches
never gave way to the violent partisanship of his colleague
in Jassy, his preference for the moderate conservative
position in all issues was clearly apparent. His fears of
the results of the violent actions of Manu and Băleanu have
already been mentioned. However, it is impossible to
judge from his reports that he had any particular prefer-
ences among the individual conservative candidates[35] or
that he in any way violated his instructions which were, after all, to remain outside of party politics. Although he continued to write of the liberals and their activities in phrases
bordering on contempt, he does not appear to have actively
worked against them. His role, if anything, in the elections appears to have been limited to that of counsellor to
the conservatives and his advice was always in the direction of extreme moderation.

Giers was also greatly concerned lest some event
cause the postponement or the eventual annulment of the
elections. When a delegation of the left came to him to request his support for their protests against the arbitrary
actions of the caimacamie and his approval of their desire
to obtain a postponement of eight days in the elections, he
refused sharply, advising them "not to compromise the
situation, which was already very delicate, by some
thoughtless action which could only harm the national cause
and to try to serve it within the limits that the convention
had assigned to the rights of the electors."[36] In answer to
the repeated complaints of the Porte on the organization of
the elections in both Principalities, Giers assured his government that the suzerain power had no just reason on
which to base its demand for the suspension of the elections.[37]

The results of the Wallachian elections to some extent
justified Giers' fears. Although the conservatives won

two-thirds of the seats, Giers was disatisfied with the results since an equilibrium was established between those
who were for Bibescu, who was the strongest conservative
candidate, and those who were against him. The latter
group included both the unionists and those of the boyars
who did not like Bibescu and who would therefore vote with
the left. Giers believed that the fission between the parties
was so great that a compromise would be impossible. Thus,
as in Moldavia, the conservatives dissipated their predominant strength in futile, factional quarrels. Moreover, the
left had captured the vote of Bucharest where the liberal
leaders Rosetti, Boerescu and N. Golescu were elected.
Giers also regretted the fact that the deputies to the assembly had been chosen with a view solely of electing a hospodar, not with the idea in mind that the same assembly
would have to revise the organic laws of the country. "The
assembly unhappily contains among its members only a very
few persons equal to that important task," lamented Giers.[38]

The three days of debates which finally resulted in the
election of Cuza in Wallachia were extremely dramatic.[39]
On January 22/ February 3 the assembly opened in the
presence of the consular corps and the high officials of the
state. Metropolitan Nifon, the president of the assembly,
called for the verification of the credentials of the candidates as the first act of the meeting. A long and animated
discussion followed. At this time and throughout the subsequent sessions the members of the left led in the debates
and were loudly supported by the crowd in the hall and by
those who had assembled in the courtyard outside of the
building. After several hours of stormy speeches, the assembly finally agreed that deputies would not be seated who
had not received a majority of votes in their district, who
had been chosen by acclamation and not by secret ballot, or
who had been elected by electoral colleges from whom electors had been excluded who had been recognized as such by
the tribunals. On this basis nine members were disquali-
fied and the meeting closed.

In the evening of the first day that the assembly met,
several members of the conservative party came to Giers
and to the other members of the consular corps to request
that they continue to attend the meetings. Their presence
was needed, it was argued, to discourage disorders and
scenes of violence.

The meeting of January 23/ February 4 was even more disturbed than that of the preceding day. The president wished to proceed with the formation of a commission for the verification of credentials, but instead the quarrels of the previous day were resumed. In the middle of the debate I. Brătianu announced the arrival of a company of militia outside of the hall. Protests were immediately made against this apparent attempt at intimidation. The news was the signal for general disorder in the hall. Public demonstrations were held both inside and outside of the building. The confusion and turmoil were so great that the president finally was forced to ask the troops to retire. He also wished to disperse the crowds outside, but this proved impossible. The assembly then again resumed deliberations "but without being able to regain either calm or dignity. Discussions followed each other without any order, deputies left their places and made injurious interpellations, the audience involved itself in the debates and the bell of the president rang in vain, covered as it was by the cries of the crowd [outside], evidently obeying orders which came to it from the hall. The sides were not equal; the intimidated majority ceded on all points."

Deeply critical of these scenes, Giers pointed out that the meeting of the second day had not advanced the questions at hand one step. The formation of the commissions was put off until the next day.

Meanwhile, the agitation and unrest in Bucharest grew. Scenes of violence occurred throughout the city, into which great numbers of people from the country had come during the meetings of the assembly. The government, in Giers' opinion, no longer had the necessary means to guarantee public security.

Since the situation now appeared dangerous, the next meeting of the assembly was held in secret session. Here Boerescu in a speech to the delegates proposed that they "vote for the hospodar of Moldavia. This decision was followed by the most enthusiastic demonstrations. Everyone was overcome with excitement and scenes of reconciliation followed the accusations and injuries." The assembly next proceeded by the prescribed rules to elect Cuza to the hospodarship.

In concluding his report on the election Giers emphasized that in the final session when Cuza was actually

elected all of the forms prescribed by the convention and
the Règlement organique had been scrupulously observed.
Despite the activities of the crowds during the previous
meetings, this session had not been subject to outside pressure. The crowd had not been allowed to fill the courtyard
before the building and had only been allowed into the assembly after the election had been proclaimed. In this despatch Giers made no comments or recommendations, pre-
ferring to give a clear account of the proceedings so that
his government could judge the situation for itself.

The double election of Cuza, which marked a liberal
triumph over the conservative majority in the chamber,
was a real victory for the Rumanian national cause and was
the principal single event in the history of the formation of
the modern Rumanian state. Although Cuza was the liberal
choice, his double election had not been the result of delib-
erate planning long in advance by his party; he had not even
been one of the leading candidates before the opening of the
Moldavian assembly. His first election in Jassy had been
brought about because of the even balance of strength between the leading liberals and because of the irreconcilable
differences between the Sturdzas. In Wallachia again it was
the split within the ranks of the leaders of both the right and
the left, coupled with the fear undoubtedly occasioned by the
agitation of the crowds in the streets and in the assembly
hall, that led all elements to rally around Cuza as the one
means of avoiding a political and social crisis.

Nevertheless, despite these circumstances, the vote of
the Wallachian assembly was a true expression of the national feeling. Both liberal and conservative abandoned his
particular preference to elect the candidate of Rumanian
union.[40] If Cuza had not so clearly stood for the national
principle, he would never have won the unanimous endorse-
ment of the assemblies. Although undoubtedly some of the
conservatives accepted Cuza with reservations and even
with the hope that the guarantor states would refuse to sanction him, the majority of the party submitted. It should be
noted in this connection that the conservatives had not
feared the unification of the Principalities and the establishment of a Rumanian state so much as the loss of political
power which such a transformation would mean to them personally. Having held absolute control in the weak and

dependent Principalities, they were not enthusiastic about sanctioning the reorganization of their country.

Popov and Giers, it will be noted, in their judgment of events in the Principalities differed in their conclusions much along the same lines that separated the liberals and conservatives. Popov, like the liberals, emphasized primarily the national issue—the necessity of supporting the Rumanian people in their struggles against foreign intrigue and oppression. Giers, in contrast, directed his attention toward the social and political conflict between the parties. Although he denounced the manoeuvres of the ultra—conservatives, because of the harm which they did to the entire party, he was personally wholeheartedly for the continuation of a conservative regime in the Principalities.

Despite the Austrian suspicions it is also apparent that the double election was in no sense a preconceived plot on the part of the French or Russian agents.[41] Although Popov and Place were genuinely sympathetic to the national movement, neither Giers nor Béclard, who were their superiors, looked with favor on the liberal position in Rumanian politics or the national movement which was under predominantly liberal sponsorship. Moreover, their official instructions specifically directed both the French and Russian agents to maintain in the Principalities the political conditions of the August convention.

The double election, a possibility not provided for in the previous agreements regulating the Principalities and in spirit against the August convention, left both Giers and Popov in a difficult situation since they were without instructions on how to proceed. In the first days Giers acted on his own initiative. His first instructions from St. Petersburg dealt with matters of procedure rather than with the general question of the attitude of the Russian government toward the personal union of the Principalities.

Notes

1. Transmitted by Giers to Popov. Giers to Popov, No. 14, Bucharest, October 10/22, 1858. An extract of these instructions was given by Kiselev to Walewski, who sent them to Béclard. The latter was instructed to associate himself with the views expressed herein. Walewski to

Béclard, Paris, October 15/27, 1858. Acte și documente, IX, pp. 104-105.

2. Popov to Giers, private letter, Jassy, September 5/17, 1858.

3. Popov to Giers, private letter, Jassy, September 26/ November 8, 1858.

4. Ibid.

5. For an account of the controversy in Wallachia and the negotiations of the powers see Riker, pp. 182-193. No attempt will be made here to discuss the attitude of governments other than the Russian.

6. Both Giers and Popov believed that the three caimacams should resume the positions which they had held in the previous administration. Popov to Giers, private letter, Jassy, September 19/ October 1; Giers to Popov, No. 17, very confidential, Bucharest, October 19/31. Béclard held a contrary opinion. See Acte și documente, IX, pp. 105-108, 124-127 and 149-150.

7. Popov to Giers, private letter, Jassy, October 30/ November 11.

8. Popov to Giers, private letter, Jassy, November 14/26.

9. Ibid.

10. Ibid.

11. Giers to Popov, No. 24, Bucharest, November 15/ 27.

12. Giers to Popov, No. 25, Bucharest, November 21/ December 3; Riker, pp. 187-188.

13. Popov, unlike Giers, formed strong personal opinions on the Rumanian leaders. In October he wrote of Vogorides: "He passes the time in orgies with his aides-de-camp; he is a real brute if there ever was one!" Popov to Giers, private letter, Jassy, October 3/15.

14. Popov to Giers, private letter, Jassy, November 21/ December 3.

15. Ibid. Popov consistently designated the conservatives as the "Austro-Turks" in the same manner that Giers

referred to the left as the "parti exalté". On the next day
Popov wrote another strong letter on the same subject. Ac-
knowledging Giers' position, he agreed that a contradictory
situation had been created in Wallachia, "but is it absolutely
indispensable always to subordinate Moldavian affairs to
Wallachian affairs no matter what the seriousness of the
first are?" Popov to Giers, private letter, Jassy, November 22/ December 4. Popov was also aware of Giers' attitude toward the left: "That party has been very cleverly
slandered. For goodness sake, do not believe that there is
a red party in Moldavia. In this respect we can be at ease."
Popov to Giers, private letter, Jassy, November 29/ December 11, 1858.

16. Ibid. Popov's despatches, which were obviously
couched in the same terms as his private letters, were subsequently read by Giers to Béclard, who noted that these
"Austro-Turks", that is, the conservatives, were precisely
the group that had aided Russia in the past. Béclard added
that when reading the despatches Giers had joked about them
and asked the French consul to excuse "the inexperience of
M. Popov in favor of his sincerity." Béclard to Walewski,
Bucharest, December 7/19, Acte si documente, IX, pp. 169-
173.

17. Popov to Giers, private letter, Jassy, December
12/24. Ten days later Lobanov wrote in a letter to Giers
a critical commentary on Popov's activities. The Porte had
complained about his attitude; "they say that he is completely under the thumb of Place." Lobanov had also received an
indirect complaint from M. Sturdza. Although it appeared
that the latter had little chance of being elected, Lobanov
thought it unwise to "burn our ships completely in case he
should become hospodar." Popov complained about the ethics of Sturdza, "but what has that to do with us? These are
certainly not models of virtue that we have before our eyes
and that we expect in the east; however that does not stop
us from carrying on business with the people in office and
from not repulsing those who have a chance of coming to
power." Lobanov to Giers, private letter, Pera, December
22/ January 3, 1859.

18. Popov to Giers, private letter, Jassy, December
27/ January 8, 1859. Previously Popov had suggested Mavrogheni, whom the Russian consul characterized as a moderate and distinguished man, as a replacement for Catargiu.
Popov to Giers, private letter, Jassy, November 22/ December 4, 1858. Place also approved Mavrogheni. See
Frédéric Damé, Histoire de la Roumanie contemporaine,
(Paris, 1900), fn. 1, p. 110.

19. R. W. Seton-Watson, A History of the Roumanians, (Cambridge, 1934), p. 263.

20. Giers to Popov, No. 25, Bucharest, November 21/ December 3.

21. Giers to Butenev, No. 26, Bucharest, November 24/ December 6.

22. On the conflict in Wallachia: Giers to Butenev, No. 27, Bucharest, November 24/ December 6; Giers to Lobanov, No. 29, Bucharest, December 8/20; Giers to Lobanov, No. 30, Bucharest, December 8/20; Giers to Lobanov, No. 31, Bucharest, December 8/20; Giers to Lobanov, No. 32, Bucharest, December 22/ January 3. These despatches also discuss the qualifications for the candidates for the hospodarship. In despatch No. 27 Giers reported that the çaimacams wanted the Porte to review the candidates for the hospodarship rather than wait for the future elective assembly, because they feared that it would sanction candidates from the left. Giers believed that this possibility should cause no concern because the electoral laws guaranteed against a preponderance of ultra-liberals in the assembly: "and in any case the danger which would result from the inscription of a hospodarial candidate from the parti avancé cannot be weighed against that which would involve a continual interference by the Porte in the internal affairs of the country ... " Giers told Béclard that he feared the activities of the ultra-conservatives rather than the ultra-liberals. Béclard to Walewski, Bucharest, October 15/27. Acte şi documente, IX, p. 106.

23. Giers to Gorchakov, No. 5, Bucharest, January 11/ 23, 1859.

24. Giers to Gorchakov, No. 3, Bucharest, January 2/ 14.

25. Giers to Balabin, private letter, January 8/20. In this letter Giers asked Balabin to communicate this information to Kiselev who apparently was not being kept fully informed on the events in the Principalities.

26. Lobanov's discussions with officials of the Porte and with the other representatives at Constantinople are recounted in Lobanov to Giers, No. 192, Pera, December 6/ 18, 1858; No. 194, confidential, December 8/20, 1858; No. 195, December 13/25, 1858; No. 205, Pera, December 27/ January 8, 1858/59. The approval of the Russian government of Lobanov's insistence that the Porte not suspend the elections on its own initiative is given in Gorchakov to

Lobanov, No. 568, December 22/ January 3, 1858/59. All of the despatches cited here are from the Russian archives.

27. From Lobanov's reports it appears that Bulwer was more enthusiastic about pursuing a drastic course of action against the caimacamies than either the Porte or the Austrian representative. Bulwer, Lobanov wrote, "after many .circumventions, and not without some hesitation, told me that, in his opinion, there was only one effective measure to take, —that was to dismiss simultaneously both caimacamies." Lobanov to Gorchakov, No. 194, confidential, Pera, December 8/20, 1859. Russian archives. Prokesch wished only the Moldavian caimacamie dismissed. Lobanov to Gorchakov, No. 195, Pera, December 13/25, 1858. Russian archives.

28. Lobanov to Gorchakov, No. 2, Pera, January 3/15, 1859. Russian archives.

29. Popov to Giers, private letter, Jassy, December 19/31.

30. Popov to Giers, private letter, Jassy, December 26/ January 7. Five days previously Popov had commented: "How will all that end? I believe that the old one [M. Sturdza] will triumph in the end." Popov believed that the unionist party was split between Lascar Catargiu, Mavrogheni and V. Sturdza. Popov to Giers, private letter, Jassy, December 21/ January 2.

31. Popov to Giers, private letter, Jassy, January 9/ 21. Popov also commented that he pitied Place who "had to smile in the face of adversity" and "accept a result which he had not at all desired but which by chance happened to be."

32. Popov to Giers, private letter, Jassy, January 16/ 28.

33. Popov thought that Place was involved with Grigore Sturdza and that he feared revelation of his conduct. Popov said that he always defended Place in public because he did not think that it was in Russia's interest to have him discredited. Popov to Giers, private letter, Jassy, January 23/ February 4.

34. Giers to Gorchakov, No. 7, Bucharest, January 16/ 28. Giers did not at all approve of Kogălniceanu's dramatic address to Cuza, which called attention to Cuza's revolutionary past, the grievances which the Rumanians had suffered in the preceding years and concluded with the hope

that under Cuza the Principalities would arrive at "that
glorious time of our nation when Alexander the Good said
to the ambassadors of the emperor of Byzantium that Rumania had no other protection than God and its sword."
Giers commented: "The levity inherent in the character of
the Moldavians makes them very easily forget all feeling of
propriety."

35. Despite Austrian suspicions there is no evidence
that Giers supported the candidacy of Filipescu. Riker, p.
202.

36. Giers to Gorchakov, No. 5, Bucharest, January 11/
23.

37. Giers to Gorchakov, No. 3, Bucharest, January 2/
14. In answer to Gorchakov to Giers, No. 557, December
19/31, 1858, requesting exact information on alleged irregularities in Moldavia and Wallachia.

38. Giers to Gorchakov, No. 6, Bucharest, January 16/
28.

39. For the details of the events leading to the double
election of Cuza see Riker, pp. 194-207. Giers' complete
account of the meeting of the Wallachian assembly can be
found In Appendix II. Béclard's report on the same event
is in Béclard to Walewski, Bucharest, January 26/ February 7, 1859. Acte și documente, IX, pp. 262-277. See also
the recent account by Dan Berindei, "Frămîntări politice și
sociale în jurul alegerii domnitorului Cuza în Țara Romînească", Academia Republicii Populare Romîne, Studii:
Revistă de istorie, VIII, nr. 2, 1955, pp. 51-73.

40. The liberal leader Ștefan C. Golescu confessed later: "We did not know Cuza and we do not know him any better today. In electing him Prince of Wallachia, after having
been elected Prince of Moldavia, we wished to make the
principle of union triumph." Ștefan C. Golescu to Paul Ba-
taillard, Paris, April 15, 1859. George Fotino, Din vremea
renasterii nationale a Tării Romanesti— Boierii Golesti,
(Bucharest, 1939), IV, p. 286.

41. Hübner, Neuf ans, II, pp. 264, 294. The suspicions
of the Austrian agents and their general lack of information
on Russian activities is reflected in the despatches published in R. V. Bossy, L'Autriche et les Principautés-Unies,
(Bucharest, 1938).

Chapter IV

RUSSIA AND THE RUMANIAN QUESTION IN INTERNATIONAL AFFAIRS FEBRUARY TO SEPTEMBER, 1859

After the double election of Cuza, Giers in his relations with the governments of the Principalities and the Russian government in negotiations with the powers followed a virtually identical policy toward the event despite the fact that Gorchakov did not send clear instructions to his agent for almost two weeks. Neither Giers nor the Russian government were enthusiastic about the election, but it was immediately apparent that it would be very difficult to suppress the results. The double election was thus conceded, but on the condition that no further steps toward union or in violation of the August convention be taken.

The issue of how far unification should proceed arose at once. On accepting his new position Cuza immediately let it be known that he was prepared to carry further the fight for real national unification. In an address to the powers he declared that he recognized the desire of the Principalities for union and a foreign prince; he would willingly retire into private life if he could thereby aid in the achievement of the national goal. Thus not only was the legality of the double election at issue, but the guarantor states were faced with the danger that further precipitant acts toward union would take place. Although without instructions, the consuls in Jassy and Bucharest were thus forced to take immediate action. The burden of decision fell principally on the French and Russian representatives because of their past relation to the Rumanian movement.

Of these Giers acted with promptness and decision to prevent further steps toward unification; Popov and Place would willingly and enthusiastically have supported Cuza in further moves.[1]   Giers at once instructed Popov to meet with Cuza, who was still in Jassy, to caution him against compromising the situation further.

In addition to his declaration to the powers, Cuza had already presented to the friendly consuls, Place and Popov, a precise program of the steps he desired to take to further the national cause. He wished to (1) convoke the Wallachian and Moldavian assemblies at Focşani and fuse them into one body, (2) name a single ministry for the two Principalities, (3) nominate at Bucharest and Jassy a director who would handle current affairs on a provisional basis, (4) form a single command for the two militias, and (5) put both provinces under a single flag.[2]   Giers' reaction to the plan was completely negative. He had already telegraphed to Popov to warn Cuza and advise him not even to attempt to proceed to Bucharest.[3]   He now instructed Popov to dissuade Cuza from carrying out the five points, which Giers believed would have little chance of support in Wallachia except from the extremists in view of the uncertain reaction of the powers. Again in this despatch he advised that Cuza not come to Wallachia for the moment since sentiment for union was strong and his appearance might add fuel to the flame. Although Giers did not oppose Cuza's fulfilling his duties as hospodar before his confirmation by the Porte and the powers, he did advise Popov to consult with Cuza on the formation of his ministry. He feared the consequences should the prince call to power members of the radical party which had been responsible for his election. Cuza was to be advised to form in Wallachia a government of moderates " equally separated from the two extremes." Of Cuza's first appointments, Filipescu and Golescu, only the former met with Giers' approval. Golescu was a forty-eighter and was strongly disliked by the conservatives.[4]

In his report on the situation to Gorchakov, Giers gave his personal reaction to the recent events. He believed that the Wallachian assembly in chosing Cuza had not wished to go beyond the achievement of personal union. He hoped that this condition could be maintained, but with the separation of the administrations of the two Principalities. He feared that the alternative, the election of a new assembly in

Wallachia or a second election by the present body, could
not be carried through without civil turmoil.[5] Since he
readily admitted the incompatibility of the double election
with the August convention, he recognized that it could only
be upheld with the express consent of the powers. He did
not want the question to be settled under any condition by
the action of the Porte alone. The election of Cuza in Moldavia had been entirely legal and should be allowed to stand
no matter what happened in Bucharest. Giers' opinion,
which reached Lobanov, Balabin, Kiselev and Titov,[6] was
that the personal union should be recognized outright, but
that in all other matters the division between the Principalities should remain. Moreover, the final decision should be
reached by agreement between the guarantor powers.

The moderate position of Giers was heartily disliked by
his colleague in Jassy. Although Popov and Place did not
act in concert and were obviously not intimate, their ideas
on the Rumanian national question were remarkably similar.
Popov was extremely disturbed by Giers' initial directions
that Cuza be advised to remain in Jassy. Cuza had originally intended to depart on February 2/14 or 3/15 for Bucharest. Popov had not shown him Giers' instructions, but "as
we are very close and I inspire in him personally more confidence than Place", he had tried to persuade the prince to
postpone his departure until further instructions had been
received. Popov reported that Cuza was being pushed by
Place and the assembly and could be held in Jassy only a
few days more. In despair he wrote, " What is to be done ?
Is all lost ? If in effect a sudden change in our policy in the
east has occured, it would be well if we were furnished with
clear and positive instructions."[7]

At the same time that Cuza was receiving these words
of warning from Russia, he also found that, despite a personal appeal to Napoleon, he could expect no support from
France in his desire to further unification. Place reported
that "twenty times " Cuza had told him that if France would
only give him some hope of support, he would proclaim
union when he arrived in Bucharest. With evident reluctance Place found himself unable to offer encouragement
since he was completely without instructions. Place was
particularly concerned about the difficult position in which
Cuza found himself, caught between the counsels of moderation of Russia and the enthusiastic desire of his countrymen

for the furtherance of the national cause.[8] Like his Russian colleague in Jassy, the French consul ardently hoped for union.

Unable to gain support from either of his patron states, Cuza bowed to necessity. He disavowed the intention of summoning the assemblies to Focşani and he acted with utmost circumspection. Nevertheless, he refused to remain in Jassy although he did delay his departure until February 8/20. He told Popov that his appearance in Bucharest was necessary to restore calm. Popov personally did not want to take the responsibility of attempting to hinder the hospodar's departure and commented that he was sure that Giers "will value him as I do and will find in him a man with whom one can come to an understanding."[9] Popov also reported the great discontent of the "ultra-unionists" in Moldavia and "their instigator, the consul of France, M. Place" with the prince's moderation.[10]

Despite this implied criticism of Place, Popov's zeal for union was quite equal to that of the French consul. In a bitter letter to Giers written on February 6/18 he called attention to Cuza's past actions, his willingness to abandon the idea of summoning the assemblies to Focşani and his moderation in other problems, which, he argued, showed the prince's respect for the wishes of the powers. Popov argued strongly against the annulling of the election in either Principality for "you do not destroy the unionist tendencies by not satisfying them, and these tendencies, constantly excited by the French agents, will end by creating a really critical situation; that is to say, what can be done today peacefully, legally, will be done later by anarchy." Russia at the future conferences should "plead openly the national cause". Otherwise the Rumanians will believe that Russia is hostile to the development of their nationality: "and that she only pretended to support union when she was sure that union would not come about."[11]

The activities of Popov were observed and commented upon by the other powers, particularly those who were not enthusiastic partisans of Rumanian nationalism. On February 10/22 Lobanov wrote to Giers that, according to a report of Churchill, Popov had appeared during a demonstration before the Russian consulate and had "shouted three vigorous hurrahs". If this story were true, Lobanov advised Giers to warn Popov in a friendly way.[12] Since the

Russian representatives did not know what was going to happen, they should adopt great reserve in language and conduct. Giers had already written in this sense to Popov on February 7/19. He did not think that Place was following the instructions of his government if the rumors concerning his activities were true. Giers cautioned again that the intention of the Wallachian assembly had been not to vote for union, but to simplify the administration through the election of a common executive. The Austrians had accused France and Russia of promoting unionist aspirations; therefore Gorchakov had instructed his agents to recommend moderation and prudence to the Rumanians until after the meeting of the projected conference.[13]

Meanwhile, after a period of silence in regard to their representatives in the Principalities and in Constantinople, the governments of France and Russia came to a decision on how to meet the double election. The Russian government was at first hesitant and Gorchakov was dubious that the act could be upheld. In a letter to Lobanov on January 26/ February 7 Gorchakov wrote that the French government had requested the Russian opinion and that: "By order of the Emperor, I replied that we would not raise any opposition, but that we will wait to learn the opinion of the other courts." Explaining the Russian attitude further, he continued:

> Although the convention of August 7/19 does not anticipate explicitly the eventuality of a double election, it is nevertheless contrary to the spirit of the Treaty of March 18/30 [1856]. There is, besides, in the convention itself article 3 which says: 'The public powers will be entrusted in each principality to a hospodar.' The powers who wish to invalidate the Wallachian election will take their stand, not without reason, on this article 3 as well as on the Treaty of Paris and we will never act against the law. We act the way we do today because we do not believe it in our interests to set ourselves up as the leader at the head of those who pursue the annulment of the Moldavian election. Nothing more, nothing less.[14]

In the following days this negative attitude shifted, but only gradually. Two days later, on January 28/ February 9, the Prussian representative in St. Petersburg, Karl von Werther, reported that Gorchakov "in confidence had

communicated unofficially that he did not believe that the
double election could be upheld."[15] In a later report Werther
added that Gorchakov had declared "sharply" against any
isolated intervention on the part of Turkey or Austria; "Russia would not be satisfied with protests against it, but would
have recourse to effective measures."[16]   However, by February 4/16 the Russian government had come to the opinion
that it would be necessary to seek the acceptance of the
powers for Cuza's victory.[17]   In a conversation with the
Prussian representative, the tsar explained the Russian
position:

> The situation in the Principalities appeared
> very serious to him, and he was of the opinion that
> it would be quite proper, considering the pressure
> of the population there for Moldo-Wallachian union,
> to maintain the double election of Cuza, in order to
> prevent greater complications on the Danube and at
> the same time to bring about union as an accom-
> plished fact. He signified thereby that he had only
> the tranquility of those lands in mind, since he
> himself did not take a further interest in union, for
> it was, besides, a measure which had been de-
> signed during the war as an anti-Russian institu-
> tion. [18]

The second letter on the double election which Lobanov
received from Gorchakov, written on February 9/21, thus
had a much firmer tone. Russia now approved the event:
"We support it," wrote Gorchakov, "as a measure of urgen-
cy, of advisability and of public order, and one which does
not affect the principle of the suzerainty of the Porte. If
the Ottoman government agrees to it, that would avoid the
gravest complications. We do not want armed intervention.
We will not participate in it in any case."[19]

Thus once again in Rumanian affairs Russia supported
the right of the Rumanian people to determine the course of
their government, even if this meant an infraction of an international agreement.[20] Cuza, moreover, had been elected
by the party of the left. Henceforth, Russia backed France
in her endeavors to obtain recognition for the hospodar.[21]
Both powers, however, were united in their opposition to
further steps toward union.[22] France's primary interest was
from now on to be centered in the Italian peninsula. Since
war was imminent in that area, neither France nor Russia
wished to risk a simultaneous disturbance in the Danubian

states. Thus both ardent promoters of Rumanian unification, Place and Popov, were warned by their governments
not to continue their sympathetic sponsorship of the Rumanian cause. In addition, Giers and Popov were ordered to
act as a brake on Cuza and to see that he proceeded with
circumspection in regard to future unionist activities and in
his relations with the Porte.[23]

The conference of guarantor powers did not open until
March 26/ April 7, 1859. Meanwhile, as we have seen,
Cuza had taken up the reigns of government in both Principalities even though he had the official sanction of neither
the Porte nor the powers. Despite the fact that the hospodar had come to Bucharest against his advice, Giers was
soon won over to Cuza personally. On February 10/22,
Giers wrote:

> Since his arrival in Wallachia Prince Cuza
> displays great activity for the maintenance of order
> and public tranquility which have been gravely com-
> promised by the past events. His attitude inspires
> much confidence and one can hope that he will know
> how to resist the influence of the parti exalté which
> wishes to see him enter upon the road of dangerous
> reforms, incompatible with the political situation
> of the country.[24]

Cuza, in Giers' opinion, had shown himself to be "firm,
resolute and of a character little susceptible of being carried away." He had taken the proper measures to ensure
order and had calmed the fears that had existed that anarchy would prevail as a result of his election. His actions
had pleased the moderate men of the country, Giers added,
but his reserved and impartial attitude toward the parties
had caused discontent among the left.[25]

Immediately after Cuza's arrival in Bucharest, Giers
held two conversations with him, the first on the day after
the hospodar's arrival in the Wallachian capital. In conformity with the moderate tone which he had adopted, Cuza
gave positive assurances that he would not go beyond the
August convention and that he would not attempt further
steps in the unification of his country at this time. Nevertheless, he appealed for Russian aid either for the confirmation of his double election, or, as a preferable alternative, for the nomination of a foreign prince and the complete
union of the Principalities. In accordance with the

instructions which he had received from St. Petersburg,
Giers repeated the advice which he had previously given on
his own account that the chambers not be united at Focşani.
Cuza replied that he would only carry through such an action
with the approval of the powers. He now also declared that
the proposed reunion had been intended only for the discussion of measures which could be adopted which would lead
to union, not for the accomplishment of the act. In the second visit, on February 11/23 Giers on instructions from
Gorchakov warned Cuza against acts of complete independence in regard to the Porte. The Russian consul considered
Cuza's assurances "too formal" to be doubted on this occasion.[26]

Although Giers was fully appreciative of Cuza's influence in calming agitation in the Principalities, he continued to feel concern over the appointments which had been
made to the Wallachian ministry from the left, particularly
that of Golescu.[27] The composition of the cabinet was a
cause of concern to the conservative party which "feared
above all the influence of the new administration in the prop
erty question, which, according to the convention had soon
to be submitted to a revision." Giers admitted that it was
difficult to judge the situation and that until the new government acted on positive measures, it would be impossible to
ascertain its intentions.[28] Nevertheless, he regretted Cuza's subsequent departure for Jassy despite the fact that he
had originally opposed the visit to Bucharest. The conservatives feared that without the stabilizing effect of the hospodar's presence, the left, the "anarchists", would promote
disorders to compromise the ministry which they could not
completely control. Giers believed that these fears were
exaggerated and were prompted by the presence of the
prominent liberals, Golescu and Brătianu, in the cabinet.
These ministers had profited by the fact that Cuza was not
acquainted with the men in public life in Wallachia to place
their adherents in district posts.[29]

Meanwhile, the powers continued to debate among them
selves the attitude which should be adopted toward the double election. The position of each was much similar to that
which it had been in the past. France remained the chief
exponent of Rumanian nationalism and stood for the recognition of the fait accompli; Russia as we have seen followed
her. The chief opposition, as before, came from Austria

and the Porte. The British attitude was negative, but the government was willing to accept a compromise. The one change was in the reaction of Prussia, where the "New Era" ministry of Schleinitz reversed the policy of Manteuffel and sought to conform its actions to those of Britain rather than Russia.[30] There was little disagreement among any of the powers on the fact that the double election was a violation of the August convention and thus of the public law of Europe. An alternative solution, however, was difficult to arrive at. The double election was obviously a reflection of the desires of the Rumanian people—a principle which had been proclaimed in previous international agreements relative to the Principalities. The action had not possessed a revolutionary character; peace and tranquility reigned in the provinces.[31]

From the beginning of the crisis it had been clearly apparent to the representatives of the powers that the election could not be undone without the use of force. The controversy over enforcement, either to annul the double election or to protect the Porte from further infringement of its rights in the Principalities should the event be recognized as an exception, dominated the diplomatic correspondence. On this question Russia was adamant. Under no condition would the Russian government accept the proposal, supported by those friendly to the Porte, that articles 27 and 29 of the Treaty of Paris be revised to allow Turkish troops to intervene in the Principalities under certain conditions without the prior consent of the powers.[32] Throughout the controversy Russia maintained the firm position that the Porte was not to be allowed to intervene to prevent the double election nor were her rights to be extended in the future.

At first, the Porte sought to gain acceptance of the idea that a unanimous resolution of the powers would be sufficient to bring the Principalities back "within the limits of legality." If not, it was argued that the intervention of a corps of Turkish troops would be enough to reestablish the previous conditions.[33] When it became apparent that the powers would not agree to armed intervention to break the double election, the Porte shifted its arguments to attempt to secure the right to enter the Principalities in the future should further violations of treaties occur. "The entire question of the Principalities is in the right of intervention," Ali Pasha, the Turkish Grand Vizier, told Lobanov.[34]

By April all of the powers, including the Porte, had come to recognize that the personal union of the Principalities would have to be accepted because of the impossibility of finding an acceptable substitute. However, it was also generally agreed that some assurance would have to be offered to the Porte that further actions toward real union would be prevented.

The conference to decide Cuza's fate opened in Paris on March 26/ April 7. At the second meeting, on April 1/13, the five powers, France, Russia, Britain, Prussia and Sardinia, presented an agreement which they had previously drawn up together. Under this plan the Porte was called upon to recognize the double election as an exception to the August convention. In an attempt to meet the Ottoman demands for guarantees for the future, it was further stipulated that should the convention be violated further, the Porte was to send a commissioner, accompanied by representatives of the guarantor powers, to the hospodar to protest. If the infraction were not corrected, the powers might advise the Porte to take action.[35]

This proposal, which signified the agreement of the majority of the powers to the double election and to personal union, was never discussed. The meetings of the conference were interrupted by an event of great European significance, the outbreak of the war for Italian unification. The Italian controversy had dominated European diplomacy throughout the winter to the almost complete displacement of the Rumanian problem which the powers believed settled by the August convention. The magnitude and nature of the issues involved in the Italian question were a great service to the Rumanian movement. The double election had indeed taken place at an historically convenient time. First, the danger of war in Italy and the outbreak of hostilities centered the attention of Europe on that peninsula. No power could afford to engage its strength in two areas. As we have seen, the chief difficulty foreseen should the powers have decided to annul the election had been that of enforcement. None of the guarantor states could spare troops nor allow his neighbor the strategic advantage of the placement of an army in the Danubian lands. Secondly, the Italian question bound Russia to France over the winter and spring of 1858-1859, the crucial period for Rumanian unification. In a series of negotiations held at the time Russia endeavored to obtain from France an arrangement whereby in return for support to French policy in the west the clauses detrimental to Russian interests in the treaty of 1856 would be annulled. The principal reasons behind the Russian support of French policy in the Principalities thus remained valid. Thirdly, the Italian war neutralized Austria, the major opponent of Rumanian nationalism. The Monarchy could not dispatch military forces to the east when they were needed in northern Italy. Fourthly, the outbreak of the war guaranteed that the Porte would not be able to take action since none of the powers wished the eastern question to arise while they were otherwise engaged.

During the time that the fighting continued in Italy, negotiations between the powers continued although Austria withdrew from formal discussions. France, backed by Britain and Russia, pressed the Porte to recognize the protocol of April 1/13. The Porte instead presented counter-proposals and discussions continued. Since Cuza's double election was not sanctioned until after the war, the hospodar's precarious position was not alleviated.

Throughout the war the Russian attitude toward the Principalities remained constant. Although the Italian issue in the long view aided the Rumanian cause, the conflict in 1859 presented certain dangers to Russian policy and, ultimately, to the independence of the Principalities themselves. It must be remembered that Napoleon's primary attention was centered on Italy; it could be expected that he would use whatever means were necessary to gain his objective there. The Russian government feared, and with justice, that France might raise the revolutionary and national elements in Galicia and Hungary against Austria. Gorchakov was also apparently worried that France might tempt Austria into trading Lombardy-Venetia for Wallachia and Moldavia. Certainly, this suggestion had already been put forth and was to be made again.[36] In a letter to his brother, M. D. Gorchakov, the governor-general of Poland, Gorchakov spoke of the danger to Russia in the Austrian acquisition of the Principalities and the necessity which Russia faced of gathering enough troops on the Moldavian frontier to occupy the country if needed.[37] Although Cuza expressed his concern to the French agent over Russian intentions,[38] as well as over those of Austria, it is clear that Russia had no designs on the Principalities except to assure that they would remain out of the hands of Austria or the Porte. Because of its preoccupation with this possibility and its intense desire that the eastern question not be reopened at this time, the Russian government was greatly concerned over the conduct of Cuza. Russia made it clear to the hospodar that she would not only support the recognition of the double election, but also that she would defend the Principalities against any foreign intervention, particularly by Turkey. Before the outbreak of the war, on March 2/14, Lobanov wrote to Giers:

> ... the rights of the Principalities will be safeguarded with respect to Turkey only by Russia who, it can be expected, will remain neutral in the Italian dispute as long as it does not take the proportions of a European war. That position will permit us to lay all of our weight on the Porte in the case that, although this is little probable, she, pushed by Austria, should wish to profit from a European complication to allow herself encroachments with regard to the Principalities.[39]

However, in return for this support the Russian government insisted that Cuza take no further steps toward unification nor was he to involve himself in the complications in Italy. As Lobanov wrote in June: "For his part, it is necessary that Cuza remain quiet; that is the condition sine qua non of our protection."[40] Repeated warnings were delivered to Cuza in this sense. He was to consider no additional moves and he was not to antagonize the Porte.[41]

Despite Cuza's repeated assurances that he would abide by the Russian desires, Giers was not satisfied with the hospodar's attitude and with good reason. Cuza greeted the Franco-Austrian conflict with real joy. On April 13/25 he wrote to his representative in Paris, Vasile Alecsandri, the Moldavian minister of foreign affairs:

> As a Rumanian, I feel the need to raise my country in the eyes of the nations and in its own esteem; as prince, I am convinced of the necessity of acting vigorously and I have decided, for the happiness and the independence of my people, to gain all the advantage possible from the events which are about to take place. The time has come to awake from that torpor which made of us an easy prize and an object of cupidity for our powerful neighbors. We have decided to throw ourselves

into the arena and to support to the limits of our power the policy of France, which is that of our prosperity and our greatness.[42]

In the same letter Cuza declared that Rumania required three things for success: money, arms and munitions, and special officers. The last item he particularly desired from France. He needed officers of all services and a general who would draw up his plans of battle. Although he had already received an indirect promise of arms from France, he confessed to Alecsandri that he hesitated to ask her for a loan.

Cuza's apparent desire and intention to profit by the war, despite his promises, aroused Giers' profound apprehension. He was particularly disturbed by two measures, taken before the outbreak of hostilities, which seemed to indicate that Cuza planned to take further action. In the first place, the prince requested from both assemblies a loan of 8,000,000 piastres (approximately 2,000,000 francs) to be raised by national subscription. Giers particularly disliked the speech justifying the loan, which emphasized its patriotic nature.

> The most prosperous, whose patriotism has been suspect until now, have today a fine opportunity to prove that they have been badly judged and that, through their social position, they wish to be the first to make sacrifices for the country. The middle classes, so proud of their patriotism, are able today to prove that their acts correspond to their words; finally the lower classes, in disposing of their slender resources, will show that they deserve the interest that we hold for them and that a nation which makes such efforts for the public good is worthy of a high destiny.[43]

The money raised by the loan was to be used chiefly to finance a camp near Ploesti where the militias of the two Principalities were to be assembled. In order to bring their number up to the 20,000 which he wished, Cuza was forced to summon all of the armed services, including the frontier guards. To replace these, he intended to organize a new force of approximately 7,000 gendarmes to police the country. The total armed strength of the Principalities would thus be considerably raised. Cuza's exact intentions in carrying out these measures were not clear to any of the foreign representatives in the Principalities. The Austrian consul, Eder, feared that Cuza wished to use the difficult situation in which Austria found herself to stir up the population of Transylvania and Bukovina.

In his meetings with Cuza, Giers was unable to obtain from the hospodar a satisfactory explanation either of the military measures or of the exact line of conduct which the Principalities would adopt in the Italian dispute. In a despatch on the question, Giers pointed out that since the Russian government was counseling Cuza in the line of moderation and respect for the August convention, there was little likelihood that Cuza would confide in him. When Béclard had discussed that imminence of war in the Italian peninsula with Cuza, the latter had not hidden his opinion that France could only encourage a movement which would force Austria to divide its forces in the coming conflict. Béclard, of course, had neither encouraged nor discouraged the hospodar. Giers warned the Russian government that it should expect Cuza to act if the proper external situation were created.[44]

In a second conversation which Giers held relative to future Rumanian actions, Cuza again gave assurances concerning his intention to unite the militias and on the national subscription. These measures, he claimed, conformed perfectly to the convention and were designed to reestablish discipline in the militia and to reorganize that branch of the administration. In regard to the war, Cuza said that he would take no step without the knowledge and direction of the Imperial Cabinet. Giers could only reiterate his advice on moderation. He argued further that it would be better not to awaken the susceptibilities of the Porte by such measures as the Ploeşti camp and the national loan before the investiture had been received. Giers also spoke of the Austrian fears and Eder's information on those in the parti exalté who wished to foment an uprising in Transylvania. Cuza replied that this story was an Austrian invention designed to compromise him before the nations. He warned that it would be a mistake for the Porte not to recognize him since the five powers had agreed to it. Should the Porte now refuse, he might be tempted to make an agreement with Serbia and throw off Turkish overlordship. Cuza in conclusion, appealed to Russia for a loan which he intended to guarantee by the state lands in the newly acquired portions of southern Bessarabia.[45]

In summing up Cuza's attitude, Giers characterized it as one of expectancy, a position which would be maintained until events allowed a change. How sincere his explanations were could not be judged, but they did not coincide with what Cuza told his intimate circle. There he openly indicated his intention of profiting from the war. If Serbia rose, he wished to join her unless stopped by the powers. He foresaw that France and Russia might go to war together and that Russia might occupy the Principalities to forestall Austria and the Porte. To prepare for this eventuality, Cuza wished to form a Moldavian and Wallachian corps, headed by French superior officers, which would act as a separate military unit along with the Russian forces. Giers discounted these plans because he thought there was little chance of their execution.[46]

In reply to this appraisal of the situation, Gorchakov drafted a long despatch to Giers which was designed to be shown to Cuza.[47] Although emphasizing the Russian concern for Rumanian prosperity and well-being, Gorchakov, nevertheless, expressed regret that Cuza had "diverged from paths of moderation which wisdom and the interest of the Principalities should commit him to maintain." He then gave a warning against French influence:

> We understand that one listens attentively to insinuations from a source perhaps equally benevolent, but less circumspect and careful, when it opens larger horizons to the mind. That is human nature and we do not wish to blame Prince Cuza, but we should call to his serious attention that in rushing into adventures one risks compromising the advantages already acquired and that the statesman should always avoid surrendering to the hazards of fortune a work which can be completed gradually owing to the force of circumstances.... All organic transformation is the work of time. To distain to take this into consideration when good landmarks are placed along the way is to act in the opposite direction of the end one wishes to obtain and to sacrifice the certain for the unknown.

In a subsequent despatch, written on May 6/19, Gorchakov continued in the same tone and condemned the reunion of Rumanian forces near Ploeşti as an expensive and pointless move.[48] Rumanian security, he emphasized, lay in the existence of the international guarantees. Moreover, the camp indicated Cuza's intention to profit from the European situation "in order to proclaim absolute independence while forming a league with neighboring populations." Giers was instructed to convey the solicitude of the tsar for "his brothers in Jesus Christ", but to emphasize that it would be regrettable "if these populations expose themselves to the hazards of fortune, on information which is not accurate or on hopes which can hardly be realized today."

Neither the loan, which was never fully subscribed to, nor the assembling of the militias, were successful measures. When Cuza attempted to summon the frontier guards they objected to leaving their villages.[49] Outright revolt broke out in some districts. Although local economic and social conditions were the primary cause for the resistance Cuza preferred to blame Russian intrigue in his conversations with Place.[50] On other occasions in the future Cuza was to use this same excuse of an alleged Russia threat to justify his activities in the face of French objections.

At the beginning of the Italian war Giers had also asked for and had received precise assurances from Cuza that he would take no action leading to an uprising in a neighboring state, a declaration which meant, of course, that the Principalities would not aid the Hungarian revolutionaries against Austria. The Russian government took formal note of the reply and emphasized its reliance on Cuza's word.[51] Neither Giers nor the Russian government thus knew of Cuza's connection with the conspiracies, sponsored by Napoleon III, involving Sardinia and the Hungarian revolutionaries.[52] Although Giers reported in his despatches rumors of the delivery of French arms to the Principalities destined for Hungary and the presence of Hungarian revolutionaries in the country,[53] he was unable to gain exact information on the question and he knew of no agreement involving Cuza directly. It was only in November, 1860 that he heard of such an arrangement, but the source was Lobanov and the details were inaccurate.[54] The quick ending of the Italian war closed any possibility of Rumanian intervention or aid to Sardinia against Austria, at least for the year 1859.

Throughout the war in Italy Russian pressure on Cuza not to attempt further actions in the national interest was paralleled by equally strong influence exerted by Russia in Constantinople to persuade the Ottoman government to

accept the April agreement immediately and without further
negotiations.[55] As in the previous months the Porte continued to employ delaying tactics. Again the question of the
right of intervention was the center of the negotiations.
However, after the defeat of Austria, the most reliable sup-
porter of the Ottoman position in the Principalities, the
Porte recognized the futility of further delay. When the
conference of Paris opened again on September 6, the powers were able to settle in a single meeting the question of
Cuza's status. The double election was recognized as an
exception and the principle of administrative separation was
reaffirmed. A complicated formula was drawn up to provide for measures to be taken should further violations of
the convention occur.[56] The only step that remained was
the formal investiture of Cuza by the suzerain power.

  With the recognition by the powers of personal union in
Cuza the major act toward the complete unification of the
Principalities had been accomplished. Russian support had
been given and had been welcomed, but it was certainly to
Napoleon III and his patronage of the national principle that
the nation owed its gratitude. Cuza and the Rumanian leaders were well aware of where their real interests lay.
They steadfastly and continuously courted France as their
chief hope of security and future progress. It is difficult to
find a more abject appeal than was contained in the words
of Alecsandri to Napoleon III: "Sire...Prince Alexandru
Ioan is devoted to you body and soul; he wishes to make of
his country a little France and he hopes only in your mag-
nanimous generosity in order to accomplish the task of the
regeneration of the Rumanian nation."[57]
  Such soft words were never so much as whispered in
Russian ears. Although Cuza would gladly have accepted a
loan from Russia, he certainly would never have considered
requesting that Russian officers train and direct his armed
forces. Despite the fact that the representatives of some
of the powers, particularly the Austrian consuls, believed
that their Russian colleagues enjoyed Cuza's confidence, it
is obvious from Giers' despatches that such was not the
case. Cuza studiously avoided frank discussions with the
Russian representatives on his present plans and his future
intentions. As we shall see in the next section, he more
often than not refused to accept Russian advice when it was
given. During the Italian war he was forced to follow the

Russian suggestions of moderation and inaction because he
was given no opportunity to act otherwise. He directly mis
led Giers on his activities in regard to the Hungarian revolutionaries. Certainly, in the next six years Cuza's actions
repeatedly belied the Austrian and even the British suspicions that he was a Russian tool.

Notes

1. In an enthusiastic despatch to Walewski on January
28/ February 9 Place signified his deep approval of the
events taking place. However, he emphasized that he had
maintained the greatest reserve in his conversations with
Rumanian statesmen and had always advised moderation
and prudence. Place to Walewski, Jassy, January 28/ Feb
ruary 9. Acte și documente, IX, pp. 277-282.

2. Giers to Gorchakov, No. 9, Bucharest, January 30
February 11.

3. Popov to Giers, private letter, Jassy, January 29/
February 10.

4. Giers to Gorchakov, No. 9, Bucharest, January 30
February 11.

5. Ibid.

6. Balabin wrote to Giers in approval of the latter's
views on the election. "Your plan is that which in my opinion presents the least disadvantages... While adding that al
though I share your idea I approve Popov, it will be easy
for you to understand me and to determine my color. I am
further of the opinion that events are stronger than men."
Balabin to Giers, private letter, Vienna, February 3/15.
Balabin sent Giers' information to Berlin, Paris, Turin,
Rome, Dresden and Stuttgart. On Kiselev Balabin wrote:
"No one is more sincerely disposed than he on the fate of
the Principalities and has for them a more affectionate re-
membrance." Balabin to Giers, private letter, n. p., n. d.
Lobanov's first reaction was that events had gone too far
and "what you tell me on the only possible solution, accord
ing to you, confirmation pure and simple of Cuza in the two
Principalities" was not possible. It was now a question of
complete union. Lobanov to Giers, private letter, Pera,
February 2/14, 1859. Lobanov's colleague, Thouvenel, be
lieved that the matter of the Principalities would continue
to be a disturbing factor until the principle of union and a

foreign prince was accepted outright. Thouvenel, Trois années, p. 337.

7. Popov to Giers, private letter, Jassy, January 29/ February 10.

8. Place to Walewski, Jassy, February 3/15, 1859. Acte și documente, IX, pp. 287-288.

9. Popov to Giers, private letter, Jassy, February 3/ 15; Popov to Giers, private letter, Jassy, February 6/18.

10. Giers to Gorchakov, No. 10, Bucharest, February 7/19.

11. Popov to Giers, private letter, Jassy, February 6/ 18.

12. Lobanov to Giers, private letter, Pera, February 10/22. When Place was also advised not to become involved in the internal affairs of Moldavia, he wrote a long and vehement denial of such activities and accused Gödel of having wrongly accused him. "For me," he wrote, "agents are only instruments who obey orders coming from above..." —a claim which is contradicted by Popov's reports of Place's activities. Place to Walewski, Jassy, February 8/20. Acte și documente, IX, pp. 289-291. Theremin also was reprimanded after the British government complained of his partisanship to union. Bloomfield to Schleinitz, February 1/13. Die auswärtige Politik Preussens, 1858-1871, edited by Christian Friese (Oldenburg i. O., 1933), I, 192, fn. 3 to document 96. This series will hereafter be cited as A.P.P.

13. Giers to Popov, private letter, [Bucharest], February 7/19.

14. Gorchakov to Lobanov, private letter, January 26/ February 7, 1859. Russian archives. Lobanov transmitted this information to Giers. Lobanov to Giers, private letter, Pera, February 7/19, 1859.

15. Fn. 3 to Doc. 132. A.P.P., I, p. 238. See also Bossy, L'Autriche et les Principautés-Unies, p. 15.

16. Fn. 1 to Doc. 139. A.P.P., I, p. 248. Russia made a similar declaration to Britain. East, pp. 165-166.

17. We have no direct documentation on the discussions that undoubtedly went on between Paris and St. Petersburg at this time. On February 14/26 Walewski sent detailed

instructions to Place and stated that the French opinion wa
identical to that which Giers and Popov had been instructe
to express to Cuza. Although the double election was undoubtedly a reflection of the desires of the Rumanians, the
should not compromise their position by further actions be
fore the meeting of the conference. Cuza had already assured Giers and Béclard that he would resist extreme mea
ures and would call for the reunion of the assemblies at
Focşani only in case of great necessity. Place was to encourage Cuza in these lines of moderation and prudence.
Walewski to Place, Paris, February 14/26. Acte şi documente, IX, pp. 292-293.

18. Werther to the Prince Regent, No. 15, St. Petersburg, February 4/16. A.P.P., I, pp. 247-248.

19. Gorchakov to Lobanov, private letter, February 9
21. Russian archives.

20. On February 6/18 Thouvenel commented on the Ru
sian attitude: "Russia is too deeply committed to disengag
herself, but I have seen, from a certain grimace of M. de
Kiselev, at the news of the double election of M. Cuza, tha
the cabinet of St. Petersburg, in gaining it is true for itsel
the honors of popularity and in winning our good graces,
does not desire any more than Austria the formation on the
Danube of a state of affairs which would guarantee Turkey
against the covetousness of its neighbors!" Thouvenel,
Trois années, p. 336.

21. The Austrian representatives were struck by the
similarity of the arguments used by Russia, France and
even Prussia in justifying the recognition of the double ele
tion: "the surprising unanimity of the wishes of the nation
the absence of a revolutionary character in that election,
the difficulty of annulling it, as well as several sophisms
which are connected with it." Koller to Buol, No. 27A, Be
lin, February 13/25, A.P.P., I, pp. 268-269.

22. Cuza's representative in Paris, the Moldavian min
ister of foreign affairs, Vasile Alecsandri, reported that
this view was urged on him in Paris. The Rumanian position was strong, he was told, because of the orderly manner by which the double election had been accomplished an
the unanimity of the votes of the assemblies. Cuza should
consider himself the ruler of two separate countries and h
should await the decisions of the conference. Alecsandri
to Cuza, Paris, February 13/25, 1859. R. V. Bossy,
Agenţia diplomatică a României în Paris, (Bucharest, 193
pp. 164-165.

23. Titov also warned that it was essential that: "the Moldavians as well as the Wallachians are able to prove by deeds their aptitude in maintaining at home public tranquility, without letting themselves be misled by the poets in politics, like M. Kogălniceanu and associates. Although it is beyond the comprehension of these gentlemen, nations make themselves respected only by the spirit of discipline and plain common sense. That is the best or rather the only basis for all social progress as for all administrative independence." Titov to Giers, private letter, Stuttgart, February 28/ March 12.

24. Giers to Lobanov, No. 7, Bucharest, February 10/ 22.

25. Giers to Gorchakov, No. 11, Bucharest, February 13/25.

26. Ibid.

27. The internal political development of the Principalities in this period will be discussed in the next chapter.

28. Giers to Lobanov, No. 9, Bucharest, February 16/ 28.

29. Giers to Gorchakov, No. 12, Bucharest, February 21/ March 5.

30. Schleinitz to Pourtales, No. 24, Berlin, February 25/ March 9. A.P.P., I, pp. 311-312. Pourtales was directed to follow the line adopted by the British representative. Since Prussia had no direct interest in the matter, the ambassador was to take no initiative.

31. Britain, in particular, was concerned over the violation of an international agreement, especially in view of the impending Italian crisis. Bernstorff reported that Malmesbury was glad that Prussia recognized that the double election was in violation of the convention and he wished the conference to state this. He objected to the French and Sardinian attitude toward treaties. Fn. 1 to Doc. 169. A.P.P., I, p. 297. Russia, who was in the process of trying to annul the restrictive clauses of the treaty of 1856, could, of course, not be moved by arguments resting on the violation of treaties. She recognized that the convention had been disregarded, but this fact alone did not justify a return to the previous condition. Kiselev, who did not favor union, wrote to his brother on February 18/ March 3: "A discord exists: on one side justice; on the other political propriety: to agree between them will be difficult. The

question must be settled with speed, and it is indispensable
to conclude it despite the reluctance of each of us to accept
on himself the initiating of similar proposals." Kiselev had
not yet received instructions from St. Petersburg. A. P.
Zablotskii-Desiatovskii, Graf P. D. Kiselev i ego Vremia,
III, p. 103.

32. Gorchakov to Lobanov, No. 85, February 26/
March 10; Lobanov to Gorchakov, No. 34, Pera, March 14/
26. Both from Russian archives.

33. Lobanov to Gorchakov, No. 16, Pera, January 31/
February 12. Russian archives. Lobanov believed that the
matter had gone too far. Even if troops entered the country
to enforce the decision of the powers, once they left the
same events would probably be repeated. Lobanov to Giers
private letter, Pera, January 27/ February 8.

34. Lobanov to Gorchakov, No. 471, Pera, February
28/ March 12. Russian archives.

35. Riker, pp. 226-227.

36. See Metternich to Rechberg, August 24/ September
5, 1859. Bossy, L'Autriche et les Principautés-Unies, pp
246-247; Hübner, Neuf ans, II, p. 238; Riker, pp. 476, 510-
512.

37. B. H. Sumner, "The Secret Franco-Russian Treaty
of 3 March 1859," English Historical Review, XLVIII (1933
pp. 65-83.

38. Place to Walewski, Jassy, May 9/21. Acte şi
documente, IX, pp. 320-322.

39. Lobanov to Giers, private letter, Pera, March 2/
14. Balabin expressed even more strongly the Russian intention to prevent foreign intervention. On March 12/24 he
wrote to Giers that the Principalities need not fear a foreign
occupation since "an aggression from whatever side it
comes would lead to war, and no one wishes it." Balabin to
Giers, private letter, Vienna, March 12/24. On May 3/15
he wrote that he hoped that the Porte would have "the wisdom not to spoil [everything] in wishing to fish in the wa-
ters that it would have troubled itself." On the question of
the right of intervention he commented: "I would counsel
the Porte neither to try nor ever to follow the visionary
dream: it is of the kind which must be drowned in blood."
Balabin to Giers, private letter, Vienna, May 3/15.

40. Lobanov to Giers, private letter, Buyukdere, June 8/20.

41. These principles of conduct are emphasized strongly in Gorchakov to Giers, No. 84, June 24/ July 6. Russian archives.

42. Cuza to Alecsandri, Bucharest, April 13/25. Bossy, Agentia diplomatica a Romaniei in Paris, pp. 165-167.

43. Giers to Gorchakov, No. 22, very confidential, April 18/30.

44. Ibid.

45. Cuza requested a loan from France through Place as well as through Alecsandri. Place to Walewski, Jassy, May 7/19. Acte si documente, IX, pp. 318-320.

46. Giers to Gorchakov, No. 23, confidential, Bucharest, April 24/ May 6.

47. Gorchakov to Giers, No. 267, May 2/14. Russian archives.

48. Gorchakov to Giers, No. 271, May 6/18. Russian archives.

49. For a recent account of the uprising see: Dan Berindei, "Framintarile granicerilor si dorobantilor in jurul formarii taberei de la Floresti (vara anului 1859)", Academia Republicii Populare Romîne, Studii: Revista de istorie, No. 3, 1957, pp. 113-133.

50. Place to Walewski, Jassy, May 9/21. Acte si documente, IX, pp. 320-322.

51. Giers to Popov, No. 34, Bucharest, May 22/ June 3.

52. Riker, pp. 269-272.

53. Giers to Gorchakov, No. 41, very confidential, Bucharest, July 11/23; Giers to Lobanov, Bucharest, No. 55, August 2/14.

54. Lobanov to Giers, private letter, Pera, November 9/21, 1860.

55. The strong position taken by the Russian government in this issue is shown in the following communications

of Gorchakov to Lobanov: telegram, secret, May 28/ June 9; private letter, June 3/15; despatch No. 338, June 4/16; despatch No. 359, June 18/30. <u>Russian</u> <u>archives</u>.

56. Riker, 248. Although the powers intended to protect the Porte against further Rumanian actions toward union, this agreement proved valueless because of the impossibility of solving the problem of enforcement.

57. Alecsandri to Cuza, Paris, February 13/25. Bossy, <u>Agenţia</u> <u>diplomatică</u> <u>a</u> <u>României</u> <u>în</u> <u>Paris</u>, p. 165.

Chapter V

RUSSIA AND THE INTERNAL AFFAIRS
OF THE PRINCIPALITIES
FEBRUARY TO DECEMBER 1859

The long delay of the powers in sanctioning the double
election was a serious impediment to Cuza in the administration of Moldavian and Wallachian affairs. He was well
aware, and his subjects continuously impressed upon him,
that he was only an interim candidate—a substitute for the
national desire for union and a foreign prince. Cuza thus
not only had to deal with antagonistic foreign powers, particularly Austria and the Porte, but he had to balance between the rival parties within his state and manage their
ambitious leaders. Because of the suddenness of his elevation to power, he had no personal following and no political organization behind him. Since knowledge of constitutional procedures and the will to adhere to them when they
were known were particularly shaky in both Wallachia and
Moldavia, Cuza could expect a period of political turmoil.
In the next year he dealt with the situation by relying largely on moderates in his administration and by refraining
from introducing positive measures on his own initiative.
The first year of his government was thus marked by a
singular lack of achievement in the reorganization of the
state institutions or in the reforms outlined in the August
convention. The blame for the negative record, however,
lies largely on the great powers who delayed their decision
for so long and on the turbulence and lack of political sense
exhibited in the legislative bodies. Even if he had so

wished, Cuza would have found it impossible to introduce and implement a strong program.

Despite the initial enthusiasm of Giers and Popov for Cuza, there was little in the hospodar's past life which seemed to fit him for the role in which he was now cast.[1] The majority of accounts picture him as cynical, indolent and weak. His personal life throughout his career was anything but ideal; he consistently showed a preference for drink and gambling over work. Moreover, he had no set principles and no definite political program to which he was attached. His qualities as a leader and a politician were thus unknown and untried. Undoubtedly, his past connections had been with the liberals; he had been a forty-eighter in Jassy and had spent a short time in exile. In 1849 he had returned and become prefect of Galatz under Grigore Ghica. In the Vogorides administration he had advanced rapidly from ensign to major in the militia in six weeks. Despite the fact that he had benefited from Vogorides' activities, he had resigned in protest against the irregularities surrounding the election of 1857. When the second elections were held, he became the deputy from Galatz to the Moldavian divan ad hoc, where he made little impression. After August 1858 he was promoted to colonel and put at the head of the Moldavian militia. Although he thus had troops at his disposal, he was not tempted to use them either for his election in Jassy or in Bucharest. His election came as a complete surprise to himself; he is said to have remarked on the event: "Gentlemen, I fear you will not be satisfied with me. Certainly, he did not possess the attribute of intense personal ambition which darkened the career of so many of his compatriots.

The convention of August 7/19 had endowed the Principalities with a political organization that would have caused chaos in nations with far more experience in constitutional government than the Principalities. The double election had added only another element to an already confused situation. The two provinces each had an assembly and a ministry. Between the two the central commission at Focşani was intended to act as a coordinating body and to draft legislation of import to both Principalities and to submit it to the respective legislatures. In order for such a system to succeed smoothly all four elements, the hospodar, the ministries, the assemblies and the central commission would need to function in harmony and to cooperate toward a common goal. In fact, the double election was only significant for the development of Rumanian nationalism if, through the uniting of two separate executive offices in one man, the two Principalities henceforth embarked on a common road of political development.

Unfortunately, in the year under consideration, from the double election of January 24/ February 5 until the end of December when Cuza was finally forced to dissolve the chambers, the total amount of practical legislation enacted by either the legislative bodies or the central commission was almost nil. Unlike his contemporaries Kossuth and Cavour, Cuza had neither been a revolutionary leader nor had he enjoyed the experience of heading a government in any capacity; he had no program to introduce and he certainly did not grasp the reigns of leadership firmly in his hands at this time. Without direction from the center the two chambers fell into political controversy and tended either to legislate on matters outside their competence or to waste time on unimportant details. The central commission went far beyond its mandate and as a result accomplished nothing of real value for the state.

The failure of the legislative bodies cannot, however, be laid on the shoulders of the hospodar. The nature of party conflicts in Moldavia and Wallachia made constitutional government difficult even under otherwise favorable circumstances. In Wallachia the conservatives dominated in number the assembly; they had approximately half the seats in Moldavia. In other words, according to the votes cast under the two class system, the conservatives held the majority in the Principalities. However, in initiative, organization and leadership the liberals had a great advantage over their opposition. In tactics they were immensely superior. Their handling of the crowds in the Wallachian assembly during the election of Cuza, in fact, the election itself, had been a victory of liberal parliamentary planning. Throughout the coming months they were to continue to hold that supremacy.

Moreover, the liberal party included in its program the measures that would have to be adopted if the Principalities were not to fall behind in their political and economic development. First, the liberals were the party of union and national liberation. Although the conservatives to some extent

supported these objectives, their attitude lacked the ro-
mantic and revolutionary appeal of their opponents and they
did not have the same aggressive attitude towards its
achievement. Second, the liberal party was, in theory, for
the equality of classes, particularly in matters of military
service and taxation. This condition was essential for the
development of a more modern and efficient state. Third,
the liberals supported the idea of land reform although with
no overwhelming enthusiasm. In fact, during the first year
their leaders made no attempt to introduce specific measures on the question. Yet for the future of the country the
abolition of servile obligations and an economically wise
adjustment of the system of land tenure were the most important internal reforms that had to be made. To the conservative this portion of the liberal program was the most
dangerous.

The conservatives had little to offer in opposition to the
liberals. They had no precise program, no real organization—and obviously no esprit de corps. Giers in his reports
constantly complained of the dominance which the left was
able to assert over the numerically stronger right despite
the fact that the conservatives had on their side their strong
social and economic position, the advantage gained by the
two class system of voting and the support of most of the
representatives of the powers. Austria disliked the liberals
because of their close associations with the revolutions of
1848; the Porte feared them as the principal instigators of
the movement toward national unification. Prussia and Britain backed conservative policies in the interest of order.
The Russian support of the conservatives, as we have seen,
was based on a preference for conservative institutions as
such and on national interest. As long as the powers had not
sanctioned the double election, Cuza was bound to heed their
opinions on matters of internal politics. He could not afford to create the fear in the minds of the neighboring powers that the Principalities would henceforth become a revolutionary center.

The policy of vacillation and opportunism which Cuza
was to follow after his election, although not ideal in theory
served well in the immediate situation. In July Giers wrote
to his wife in disgust, "Cuza is a scoundrel of the worst
kind—he promises everything and does nothing."[2] By meeting pressure from without by this method, "by promising

everything and doing nothing," Cuza was able to guard his
own position and the independence of the state. Giers was
not at all hesitant about issuing advice. As has been seen,
he had already instructed the hospodar on how to act after
his election. In the succeeding months the Russian consul
pressed constantly for conservative appointments and conservative ministries in both Principalities. Since Cuza had
been elected largely through liberal support and since the
liberals were by far the more vocal and troublesome of the
two parties, Cuza could not afford to ignore them even if he
had been so inclined.

Cuza's first appointments were a compromise. In
Wallachia, where the conservatives dominated the assembly,
he appointed the conservatives B. Catargiu and I. Filipescu
and the liberals N. Golescu and D. Brătianu to the ministry.
In Moldavia V. Sturdza, the former caimacam, was placed
at the head of the government. Of the two, the Wallachian
chamber proved the more refractory. The assembly immediately came into conflict with the liberal ministers, who
in turn quarreled with their conservative colleagues. In
March Brătianu went to Jassy to try to persuade Cuza to
dissolve the Wallachian assembly in the hope that new elections would produce a liberal victory. Giers advised Popov
to argue strongly against such a move; he feared that dissolution would have bad effects in the country and that the agitation aroused would influence adversely the attitude of the
powers. When Popov reported the success of his efforts,
Giers was delighted. He had not yet abandoned his early
favorable impression of Cuza and regarded his negative decision on dissolution as a "witness of the soundness of judge-
ment and the firmness of which Prince Cuza has already
given so many proofs since his double election to the hospo-
dariat. . . ."[3] After expressing the opinion to Popov that it
would be best if Cuza abandoned Golescu and Brătianu, but
retained the conservatives in his ministry, Giers left the
manner in which this should be approached up to Popov:
"abandoning to your tact the use that you believe that you
can make of this view with the hospodar."[4]

Despite counsels of moderation from the Russian, Prussian and French consuls Cuza felt forced to take action.[5]
After the conservative assembly passed a vote of no confidence in the ministry, a move aimed solely at the liberal
members, Cuza decided to make a clean sweep and not only

dismissed Golescu and Brătianu, but also Catargiu and Filipescu. Giers lamented that the last dismissals were a
disaster and believed that Cuza had provoked the crisis
gratuitously. Cuza, he complained, did not want to rely either on the liberals or the conservatives, confounding the
latter with the partisans of the former hospodars. He
wanted only moderates, but he was not acquainted with the
men in the country. If he had realized the difficulty of finding suitable candidates for public office, he would have assured himself of the services of Filipescu and Catargiu for
a lifetime! Now he was dominated by his fear of the conservative majority. Even though the Russian, Prussian and
French consuls had cautioned him, he had refused to change
his decision. The new ministry, formed by Nicolae
Crețulescu, belonged to neither party in the chamber, but
Giers commented that "it is to be doubted whether it is up to
the height of the situation."[6] The assemblies then went into
recess until May.[7] In the meantime, a comic opera episode
took place.

On April 3 Giers reported to Gorchakov the details of
what was apparently a plot against the life of Cuza.[8] It appeared that soon after the election of the prince and at the
time of his first visit to Bucharest, Gigiano, a conservative
deputy, was approached by a Jewish tailor named Bernard
Schenk with a proposition. Schenk told the deputy that he
knew of some foreigners who had recently arrived in Bucha
rest and who were busy making an "infernal machine" for a
yet unknown purpose. Posing as a partisan of the members
of the old regime whose interests had been injured by Cuza'
advent to power, Schenk proposed that Gigiano use the men
and their bomb to get rid of Cuza. Gigiano immediately reported the affair to Cuza, who turned the matter over to the
police. In the course of the investigations which followed,
Gigiano, assisted by another police agent, acted as an agent
provocateur. When it appeared that the conspiracy was full
organized, the police seized seven of the men who were involved in the affair. These included Schenk, a German me-
chanic named Joseph Green, one Galician and four Croatian
all were Austrian subjects. Among the papers seized, two
proved incriminating. The first was an engagement, written in German, that the assassins would finish off their vic-
tim with a gun or a knife if that should prove necessary.
The second contained the sentence, "the hotbed is at

Constantinople, the smoke at Galatz, and the fire at Bucharest."

This, then, had apparently been a serious threat to the prince.[9] On April 10/22 Giers was forced to write a second despatch reporting the results of a further investigation of the plot. It appeared that the whole affair had started only as a "bad joke" on the part of Schenk who wished to extort some money from Gigiano. Only after the police agent, Bobiglio, entered the picture had any kind of a conspiracy developed. Not only had Bobiglio directed the construction of an "infernal machine" after his own design, but he had drawn up the agreement with the conspirators. He had recruited the four Croatians and paid them with police money. Unfortunately, in putting Bobiglio on the case his superiors neglected to inform him of Gigiano's revelations. Bobiglio had thus directed all of his energy toward compromising the poor deputy who in turn was also acting as an agent provocateur.[10]

In May the assemblies again convened. By this time both Popov and Giers, who it must be admitted had so far had relatively little success in influencing the prince, had come to hold a lower opinion of Cuza. On May 15/27 Popov wrote to Giers in excuse of Cuza's actions: "Besides, one must recognize that his position is very difficult and made to embarrass a stronger head than his: no moral support, no credit, no material resources; almost everyone as an enemy; in the eyes of the old he is not conservative enough, in the eyes of the young not progressive enough. And then the jealousies, the repressed ambitions!"[11] In commenting on the general situation in a report to Gorchakov, Giers wrote in a similar pessimistic vein, but added that no matter how different the principles and beliefs of the opposing groups in the assembly and the central commission were, all wished to get out of the present situation:

> Some are not satisfied with the result obtained by the double election, believing the moment favorable to obtain the complete union of the two countries and perhaps even their political independence, others regret the past and, having no confidence in the present regime which keeps all the classes of the population in turmoil, are ready to join together under the banner of the parti avancé only in order to compromise the situation to the point of necessitating a more effective

> intervention of the guaranteeing powers and to
> prove to them that the parliamentary regime
> granted by the convention is still inapplicable in
> these lands.[12]

Giers believed that the situation had been made worse
by the Paris conferences and by the "inexperience and ver-
satility" of Cuza, who at first had shown himself so "firm
and energetic". Giers was also concerned about the constant change of ministers and secondary officials.[13]

Once in session again the Wallachian chamber com-
menced the favorite occupation of the legislatures of the
Principalities, that of examining the record of their prede-
cessors, and began an examination of the accounts for the
past three years.[14] The principal point at issue was the
administration of Prince Ghica, whom the conservatives
wished to force to restore some of the money spent during
his administration. He had evidently used public funds to
try to gain the position of hospodar. The left, who defended
Ghica with a "remarkable tenaciousness", insisted that if
Ghica's accounts were investigated, the assembly should ex-
amine all since 1847. Although sympathetic to the conservatives, "who had such just grievances against the ex-caima-
cam Alexandru Ghica",[15] Giers deplored the entire episode
as completely illegal. He objected particularly to the decision to go over the accounts as far back as 1847, a period
which involved principally the seven year administration of
Ştirbei. The latter had written to Cuza from Paris and
Giers strongly supported his arguments. Cuza agreed with
Giers on the illegality of the investigation and promised that
he would refuse all assistance in putting the plans of the assembly into effect. If the executive power did not cooperate
the decision of the assembly would have no practical result.
Giers believed that Cuza and his ministers were being
forced to use care with the "men of 1848", but that this
"harmful" system would be abandoned once the powers recognized him. "Until then," concluded Giers, "we will have
I fear, to report many irregularities in the course of events
here as well as in Moldavia."[16]

The Wallachian assembly closed on July 4/16 having
accomplished little since a great part of the measures it did
pass belonged within the jurisdiction of the central commission. Commenting on its work in a long report,[17] Giers
particularly pointed out how "the Wallachian assembly has

lost no time adopting the equalitarian principles laid down
in Article 46 of the convention of August 7/19" and had accepted the principle for military service that "every Rumanian, without distinction of class, designated by lot, is a
soldier." The adoption of a personal tax which fell on all
equally also belonged in this category. During this session
of the assembly, Giers continued, the ministry of Crețulescu
had achieved little more success in conciliating the divergent groups than had its predecessor. The liberals, under
their spokesman I. Brătianu, had kept up a constant barrage
of criticism. When the government's budget came up for a
vote, it was accepted with only a few changes, but, Giers
wrote, only after a most stormy and personal discussion.
In this debate Brătianu declared that he had voted for it "only in order to sustain the act of January 24 but that it was in
no way evidence of his confidence in the government, which
since January 25 had lost so much time without doing anything." When Brătianu again criticised the ministry at the
close of the session, Crețulescu asked for a vote of confidence. Brătianu assured him that he had already received
this when the assembly accepted the budget; a further vote
might call into question the election of January 24. The
members of the left walked out of the hall crying "vive l'élu
du 24 janvier!"[18] The liberals thus attacked the ministry,
but they feared to compromise the double election.

Giers, as could be expected, was very critical of the
actions of the assembly. Only a few of its decisions could
be put into effect. "During the entire session," he commented, "the attitude of the chamber has been rarely worthy
of its high mission,—the parti exalté although in the minority almost always succeeded in dominating it." The conservatives had made little effort to stop them. "It is not even
impossible that in letting the men of 1848 alone the conservatives have had in view the further compromising of the situation which appeared intolerable to them."[19]

By September, when the double election was recognized
by the powers, Cuza had thus been unable to form a stable
administration. To the political difficulties was added the
threat of economic disaster. In August the prolonged heat
of summer foretold a bad harvest. "The harvest this year
will be non-existent ... all is perishing," reported Popov.[20]

In October when the assemblies were not in session,
Cuza proceeded to take several measures to ensure calm in

the country.[21] These were put through as simple ordi-
nances of a provisional character or old regulations were
revived. Public assembly was forbidden and a system of
warning and restriction was imposed on the press. Giers
now strongly urged Cuza to make further changes in his
ministry. He felt more than ever that the country needed a
government which could assure a regular, orderly development under the new constitutional procedures; the Creţulescu
ministry had been completely disorganized. Only the conservatives could provide the necessary leadership.

Despite Giers' advice Cuza replaced the ministry of
Creţulescu with one headed by I. Ghica and A. Golescu. The
prince told Giers that he wished to rely on moderates who
did not belong to either of the parties which divided the assembly.[22] Giers noted that although some of his colleagues
approved the choice, he personally did not agree. Ghica
and Golescu could only succeed if they gave the majority in
the ministry of seven to the conservatives, who held also
the majority in the chamber, but this had not happened. Un
der the circumstances Giers did not see how the ministry
could accomplish its tasks, deprived of the support of the
assembly, and, in Giers' opinion, devoid of knowledge of the
real state of the country. During the ministerial crisis,
which had lasted some days, Giers in his conversations with
Cuza:

> never ceased repeating to him that according to
> my opinion no combination would be able to succeed
> without the predominant participation of the con-
> servatives who enjoy the reputation which they
> owe to their social position, their experience in
> affairs and finally the majority in the chamber,
> with which every constitutional government must
> necessarily reckon.[23]

Giers assured Gorchakov that the main reason that he
had spoken so emphatically was that he believed that only
with a conservative administration could success be achieve
in the question of the Dedicated Monasteries, since the conservatives in Wallachia were less hostile to the interests of
the Greek clergy than were the liberals.[24] Ghica had also
won Giers' dislike as an apparent British partisan.[25]

At the same time that Cuza had assumed the executive
power in both Principalities, he had also proceeded to implement another portion of the August convention, that

concerning the establishment of a central commission at Focşani. Although he had been dissuaded from uniting the assemblies, he was nevertheless determined to establish the commission. When Giers learned of this intention, he transmitted to Popov instructions to try to deter the hospodar from any further actions tending toward union.[26] The disadvantages of waiting were momentary and such a move at the time might compromise the recognition of the double election. The conference would soon meet and the powers should not be faced with another problem. Upon receiving this advice, Cuza told Popov that he could not delay further. Despite the fact that Place and Béclard backed Giers, Cuza continued with the appointments to the commission.[27] According to the convention, the commission was to be composed of sixteen delegates, half from each Principality. Of these eight were appointed by Cuza and eight by the assemblies.

The entire question of the commission immediately became another issue in the struggle between the political parties. Under the inspiration of the unionists the Moldavian assembly refused to vote salaries to its representatives on the argument that the Principalities had already declared themselves for union and a foreign prince; salaries could be determined later and in proportion to the service which each individual member had rendered to the cause of union.[28] Popov commented:

> Do I need to tell you that the final word of the affair is this: to put a spoke in the wheels of Cuza's government and to make him continually change his ministry? Also I believe that what the prince should do immediately after he is confirmed is to dissolve the assembly which, with a few exceptions, is composed only of muddlers.[29]

The Wallachian delegates, in contrast, were voted a salary.

The final appointments made to the commission by the hospodar, which were Epureanu, Grigoriu, Malinescu, and Teriaki in Moldavia and Golescu, Predescu, Arghiropulo and Tell in Wallachia, were no more pleasing to Giers than the decision to proceed with the appointments.

> ... this choice, made principally in the most advanced party, is quite unfortunate and will present,

> in my opinion, great disadvantages because of the
> incompatibility of the ideas and political principles
> of the members of the commission named by the
> hospodar and those who are delegated to it by the
> two elective assemblies.[30]

On May 11/23 Cuza opened the meeting at Focşani with
a speech which caused Giers to comment that, although it
did not impose directly the duty of accomplishing union, it
nevertheless indirectly indicated the desirability of such action. Again Giers stressed the importance of the immediate recognition of Cuza in order to calm the unrest in the
country. Giers also expressed his fears about "the too advanced tendencies which for some time have been manifeste
even among the most timid members of the committee of
Focşani."[31]

As Giers had expected, the central commission proved
to be anything but a body calming to public opinion or bene-
ficial to the establishment of stable government in the Principalities. The question of union and a foreign prince, an
issue which was entirely out of the competence of the body,
was immediately taken up. The initiative for the measure,
to Giers' dismay, came from the conservative party under
the leadership of G. Sturdza. The intention of the party was
to gain the acceptance of the idea that until the national desire for union was achieved "all deliberation on the question of internal reforms" would be postponed. The progressives countered with the demand that laws be drawn up at
once to comply with the convention, particularly with the
"equalitarian dispositions" of Article 46. The question of
union could be then considered. The even division of the
parties in the commission resulted in a deadlock. Both
groups were obviously acting outside of the political framework given them by the powers and against the policies favored by the Russian government.

The action of the conservatives had been a direct attack
on Cuza, who now showed increasing signs of desiring to
confide the administration to the left. Giers again used his
influence to try to deter Cuza from this "dangerous project.
He blamed the conservative stand, which he agreed was
mistaken, on "the disquiet which the reforming inclinations
of the parti avancé inspires in them in the indecisive situation of the moment."[32]

The commission in the next month continued its

deliberations and in great secrecy proceeded to draw up a constitution. Discontent with Cuza's administration was apparent throughout the country during this time. The commission continued to base its work on the idea of the complete unification of the Principalities under a foreign prince, a condition declared essential for the application of the new organic statute drawn up at Paris. The legislation which was being considered at Focşani was also based on this principle. Since the carrying out of the August convention depended on the cooperation of the central commission and the two assemblies in legislation, Cuza's government, based on union through a common hospodar, was in a sense functioning without a base.

Giers did not approve at all of the direction of conservative policy in the central commission and the espousal of union and a foreign prince. The progressives were now the ardent supporters of the elections of January 24, because, Giers wrote, "the men of the extreme party do not wish to hear of a foreign prince who without a doubt would inaugurate a system of order and of discipline and would make the government stronger than it is under the present regime." Giers feared that the conservative proposals, which could never be carried into practice, would only lead to a rapprochement between Cuza and the left which would be to "the detriment of the real interests of the country." Giers again expressed the belief that the major difficulties arose from the Porte's delay in granting the investiture. If this had been done in time, Cuza would probably have been kept on the road "of wisdom and of moderation, which he had adopted on his assumption of power."[33]

When Giers met Cuza at Ploeşti, the prince confirmed the fact that the majority in the central commission supported the appointment of a foreign prince, but that they hesitated to act because of the impending meeting of the conference of Paris. Cuza at this time went out of his way to assure Giers that he would not tolerate "any deviation from the limits set by the convention of August 7/19" and that after the arrival of the firman of investiture he would approach the conservative party and make a choice of enlightened men to whom he would confide the administration. Giers did what he could to influence Cuza in this direction, but from his experiences of the last few months he saw that he could not put too much trust in the assurances of the hospodar, "whose character, quite honorable though it is, unfortunately distinguishes itself by a regrettable inconstancy. "[34]

On November 14/26 Giers was finally able to send to St. Petersburg an unofficial draft of the constitution drawn up by the central commission. He commented that he feared that the document which he sent would have to be considered as authentic, despite its adventurous spirit "about which one cannot be astonished enough considering that the majority of the members of the central commission belonged to the conservative party. "[35] The constitution was based completely on the principle that the two Principalities were to be considered as a single independent state according to the wishes expressed by the two divans ad hoc of 1857, with no reference to the August convention or to the other decisions of the powers affecting the provinces. The prince was envisaged as an independent ruler; he could coin money, confer decorations, make agreements with foreign governments, etc. His powers, however, were greatly restricted and he had to pledge himself to maintain the "very democratic" constitution. Henceforth, Bucharest was to be the capital of the country. Giers was also critical of the fact that the administration and the judiciary were to be organized on French models, which Giers did not think conformed to the state of civilization of the country.[36]

When Cuza received the constitution, he was not certain how it should be handled. It was a direct blow at his government since it was based on real union and not on the election of January 24/ February 5. At first, he told Giers, he had intended not to reply to the communication of the commission because he had already decided to dissolve the assemblies and the central commission. Giers urged the prince to make a statement upholding the August convention as the basic document determining the political organization of the Principalities. The decision to dissolve the assemblies and the commission met with Giers' full approval; he reported that he agreed with Popov that the mandate of the assemblies had been to elect chiefs of state. Now the government could ask the nation to elect purely legislative bodies. Although Cuza expected that new elections would be favorable to him, Giers expressed some doubts on the probable results.[37]

Faced as he was by two legislative bodies who were unable to cooperate with the ministries and by the work of the central commission, which had acted outside of its legal limits, Cuza had little choice but to call for new elections and hope that the country would support him at the polls. Cuza's first year as ruler of the Principalities had thus been far from successful in domestic politics. Although he had gained recognition for the double election from the guarantor powers, he had been unable to form a stable government in the Principalities or to take advantage of the institutions given to the country.

During the year it had also become quite apparent that in electing Cuza as the single executive of both provinces, neither the liberals nor the conservatives had any intention of allowing him real power or of surrendering the leadership of the government to him. He was intended to fill the role of a regent until circumstances allowed the choice of a foreign prince. Left to his own decision, Cuza would have, undoubtedly, formed a liberal ministry, but before Russian pressure and the fact that the conservatives dominated the assemblies, he was forced to try to find a middle course. Of the three Wallachian ministries formed before the dissolution of the chambers, none was able to put through a positive program or to control the irrational acts of the central commission. However, despite Cuza's lack of success in domestic affairs, the year 1859 marked a great achievement for the Rumanian national cause. Not only was Cuza elected in both provinces, but, equally important, he was recognized by the Porte and the guarantor powers although their assent signified a violation of the agreement of 1858.

Notes

1. On Cuza see Paul Henry, L'Abdication du Prince Cuza et l'avènement de la dynastie de Hohenzollern au trône de Roumanie, (Paris, 1930), pp. 2-4; N. Iorga, Geschichte des Rumänischen Volkes, (Gotha, 1905), II, pp. 312-314; Riker, pp. 196-197; Seton-Watson, p. 301; and A. D. Xenopol, Istoria Românilor din Dacia Traianǎ, (Bucharest, n.d.), XIII, 7-23.

2. Giers to Olga, private letter, Bucharest, July 7/19, 1859. It is interesting to note that the identical comment was made three years later by the mother of the prominent Golescu brothers concerning Cuza's treatment of the liberals. She wrote: " . . . for we already know the instability of character of our man, who always promises and doesn't do

anything. How many times has he beguiled us, we liberals, with soft words in assuring us that he also is of the national party, that he also has been persecuted, expatriated by the reactionaries ... " Zoe C. Golescu to Ştefan C. Golescu, n.p., February 15/27, 1862. Fotino, Boierii Goleşti, IV, p. 376.

3. Giers to Gorchakov, No. 14, Bucharest, March 7/ 19; Giers to Popov, No. 12, Bucharest, March 7/19.

4. Ibid. In this chapter only the internal politics of Wallachia will be discussed since Giers did not deal with Moldavian affairs in detail in his despatches. After the double election Popov's letters become less frequent so they are not an adequate source for developments in Jassy. In general, however, Cuza's administration in Moldavia faced the same problems as that in Wallachia. Here too the prince was forced to change his ministry three times during the year.

5. Giers to Gorchakov, No. 18, Bucharest, March 27/ April 8.

6. Ibid.

7. Giers to Lobanov, No. 20, Bucharest, March 30/ April 11; Giers to Gorchakov, No. 20, Bucharest, April 3/ 15.

8. Giers to Gorchakov, No. 19, Bucharest, April 3/15. See also Xenopol, Istoria Românilor, XII, 314-315, for a different version of the affair.

9. On April 3/15 Popov wrote to Giers requesting details on the reported assassination attempt, commenting: "Imagine, the unionists wished to propose to the chamber to proceed in corpore to Bucharest in order to congratulate the prince!! You understand their real aim. The comedians!" Popov to Giers, private letter, Jassy, April 3/15.

10. Giers to Gorchakov, No. 21, Bucharest, April 10/ 22.

11. Popov to Giers, private letter, Jassy, May 15/27.

12. Giers to Gorchakov, No. 25, Bucharest, May 8/20.

13. Ibid.

14. See Riker, pp. 244-245.

15. Giers to Gorchakov, No. 37, Bucharest, July 3/15.

16. Giers to Gorchakov, No. 42, Bucharest, July 17/29.

17. Contained in Giers to Gorchakov, No. 39, Bucharest, July 11/23.

18. Ibid.

19. Ibid.

20. Popov to Giers, private letter, Jassy, August 8/20. Giers wrote to his wife on the same day about the bad conditions in the country: "thus one hears on all sides only complaints." Giers to Olga, private letter, Maya, August 8/20.

21. Giers to Gorchakov, No. 61, Bucharest, October 10/22.

22. Giers to Gorchakov, No. 62, Bucharest, October 17/29.

23. Giers to Gorchakov, No. 61, Bucharest, October 10/22.

24. Ibid.

25. Giers to Gorchakov, No. 62, Bucharest, October 17/29.

26. Giers to Popov, No. 16, Bucharest, March 13/25; Giers to Gorchakov, No. 15, Bucharest, March 13/25. Popov did not agree. He believed that although the "Austro-Turks" might object, it was not logical to contest Cuza's right to appoint members to the commission when it was part of his right to govern the Principalities. Russia had, after all, supported his immediate assumption of executive power even without recognition by the Porte. Popov to Giers, private letter, Jassy, March 20/ April 1.

27. Giers to Gorchakov, No. 16, Bucharest, March 21/ April 2. Cuza explained his action to Place as follows: "It is evident that we are going to perish for lack of provisions if I do not give some sign of life, and I cannot do better in order to reassure the restless country than to proceed with the formation of the central commission which is the point of departure for the putting into practice of our reorganization." Place to Walewski, Jassy, March 22/ April 3. Acte şi documente, IX, pp. 305-306.

28. Giers to Gorchakov, No. 18, Bucharest, March 27, April 8. In a report on the meeting of the Moldavian delegates, Place wrote that a deputy had argued that payment should not be decided upon since if the members of the commission did not proceed on the basis of unity "they didn't deserve five paras" and if they accomplished the task the country would "reward them amply." This deputy was chosen by the assembly to sit on the commission and his motion passed by a large majority. Place to Walewski, Jassy, March 25/ April 6. Acte şi documente, IX, p. 310.

29. Popov to Giers, private letter, Jassy, March 27/ April 8.

30. Giers to Lobanov, No. 23, (Bucharest), April 11/2

31. Giers to Gorchakov, No. 27, Bucharest, May 16/28

32. Giers to Gorchakov, No. 32, Bucharest, June 13/2

33. Giers to Gorchakov, No. 44, (Bucharest), July 24/ August 5.

34. Giers to Gorchakov, No. 45, Bucharest, July 31/ August 12.

35. Giers to Gorchakov, No. 67, Bucharest, November 14/26.

36. Ibid.

37. Giers to Gorchakov, No. 69, Jassy, November 30/ December 12. On the dissolution of the central commission Lobanov commented: "No matter what it is, I am, for my part, delighted with the resolution of Cuza, for, frankly, the work of the committee of Focşani hasn't any common sense." Lobanov to Giers, private letter, Pera, November 23/ December 5, 1859.

Chapter VI

LOCAL CONFLICTS: THE DEDICATED MONAS-
TERIES, CONSULAR JURISDICTION AND
THE BESSARABIAN REFUGEES

After the double election of Cuza in January 1859 the
Russian government engaged in a series of controversies
with the Principalities on matters involving the Russian
position in the country and Russian rights under the treaties.
Among these were the questions of the Dedicated Monasteries, consular jurisdiction, and the treatment to be accorded to inhabitants of Bessarabia wishing to migrate to
Russia in conformity with the provisions of the treaty of
1856. Of these the affair of the Dedicated Monasteries assumed an overwhelming importance; it is this problem
which dominates all others in Russo-Rumanian relations in
Giers' despatches.[1]

It has previously been mentioned that in her relations
with the Balkan nations Russia's community of faith in the
Orthodox church with these people was a point of strength.
This condition, however, was not true in the Principalities
where Russian support of the oecumenical Orthodox church
brought Russia into conflict with Rumanian national sentiment. The Rumanian church, like its counterparts throughout the Balkans, was subordinate to the patriarchate of
Constantinople. Wallachia and Moldavia formed separate
metropolitanates with their centers at Bucharest and Jassy.
The higher clergy resided in the capitals and devoted its
principal attention to its political functions; its members
served the state as administrators, judges and in a legislative capacity. The bishops were dependent on the

Patriarch of Constantinople in that his approval was necessary for their appointment. The Rumanian church was thus
as much a political as a religious institution. In common
with the leading organs of administration in the Principalities, corruption was widespread. The church was, moreover, separated from the mass of the population and, from
all accounts, had little direct hold on the people.

The principal significance of the Rumanian church was
neither political nor spiritual, but economic. In Moldavia
a quarter of the acreage and in Wallachia a third was held
by the monasteries. These institutions were intended to
supply general social services, such as schools and hospitals, as well as to serve religious functions. They were di
vided into two categories. The first, those who were not
dedicated, caused no difficulty because their superiors wer
native and they were subordinate to the state. The second,
the Dedicated Monasteries, are those of the greatest interest. These institutions were "dedicated" to various Hol
Places, such as Mt. Athos, the monasteries of Jerusalem,
and the Patriarchates of Constantinople, Jerusalem, Alexandria and Antioch. Their superiors, or hegumens, were
appointed from the Holy Places to which they were dedicated and were normally Greeks. These monasteries paid
no taxes and were not under the control of the state. Their
property had been acquired through the bequests of individuals who had usually stipulated that the income of the land
donated should be used for local charitable purposes with
only the surplus going to the Holy Places. The latter, how
ever, in the nineteenth century took the position that they
owned the lands outright and could dispose of the income as
they saw fit. As a result the hospitals, chapels and other
works under their control fell into ruin. Moreover, the
Holy Places became increasingly dependent on the revenues
from the Dedicated Monasteries for their support.

The existence of this vast domain, out of the control of
the state, was always an obvious source of grievance for
the governments of the Principalities.[2] From 1821 onward
successive governments attempted to meet the problem and
lay their hands on this rich source of revenue. Unfortunately, the task was difficult to accomplish. The Greek
hegumens, resisting all attempts of the Principalities to
gain control over them, considered themselves either Russian or Ottoman subjects. Through their prestige as the

representatives of the Holy Places and through the corruption they so freely employed, they fought to maintain their absolute independence. Their ability to hold their position was due primarily to the unstinted support which they received from Russia.

Although the Dedicated Monasteries had undoubtedly aided Russia in her occupations of the Principalities, when they had served as centers of intelligence and had provided supplies to the armies, Russian support of these institutions was closely joined to her interest in maintaining the strength and prestige of the oecumenical Orthodox church. Through this question, where Russian sanction was thus indirectly given to practices which were corrupt and unjust, Russia separated herself successively from three elements of the Rumanian people—the clergy, the peasant and the boyar. The Rumanian higher clergy naturally resented the influence and power of the non-national institution which was in no way under the influence of the Rumanian ecclesiastical authority. The peasant saw that those who worked the estates of the Dedicated Monasteries received worse treatment than those on private lands. The great boyar, ever eager to increase his estates before a rising grain market, coveted the vast estates of the church. Although certain boyars made handsome profits by taking the contracts for the collection of revenue on the monastic lands, it was the great landowners who led the attack. After 1830 they began in earnest; they demanded investigations and a study of the original donations under which the monasteries acquired their lands. In joining herself with intensity and conviction to the defense of the monasteries, Russia found an issue on which there was little division of opinion among the social classes and political parties in the Principalities; all sought an end to foreign jurisdiction over so large a part of their territory.

With Russian backing the Greek clergy initially was able to withstand the demands of the Principalities. However, in 1843, although still refusing to contribute from the revenues of the Dedicated Monasteries on a proportional basis, the Greek church agreed to pay annually a fixed sum of a million piastres for nine years. At the end of this time another sum was to be agreed upon based on the revenues. In return, the monasteries were freed from certain troublesome interferences from the civil

authorities. Bibescu, disatisfied with the arrangement, re
fused the money, but Sturdza accepted 500,000 piastres for
Moldavia. After 1851 the revenues of the monasteries were
handled by tax farmers who held nine year leases, the con
tracts being awarded by public auction. In 1851 and 1852
the Russian government initiated new negotiations between
the hegumens and the patriarchs which failed to lead to any
agreement. During the Crimean war, in an attempt to set
tle the matter to their own satisfaction while Russia was
otherwise occupied, the Principalities requested the Porte
to impose on the eastern church a settlement involving a
surrender of a proportion of the revenue. Moldavia requested a fourth, Wallachia a third. Although the sultan
named a commission, it could not act since it did not have
the original acts of donation through which the funds were
dedicated to the Holy Places. The question was taken up
again at the Conference of Paris where at the instigation o
Russia the following procedure was outlined in Protocol
XIII.

> The interested parties shall be invited to
> come to an understanding among themselves by
> means of a compromise; in case they do not suc-
> ceed in coming to an understanding in a year's
> time, it will be settled by means of arbitration.
> In case the arbiters do not succeed in coming to
> an understanding, they will chose an over-arbiter.
> If, in turn, they find it impossible to agree on the
> choice of this over-arbiter, the Sublime Porte
> will confer with the Protecting Powers for the
> purpose of designating one.[3]

When no further steps were taken leading to an agreement, the Wallachian government in the spring of 1859 too
a radical step and announced its intention of sequestering
a fourth of the revenues of the monasteries, threatening
with expulsion the hegumens who did not comply with the
order. On April 24/ May 6 Lobanov telegraphed to Giers
the complaint of the Patriarchate of Jerusalem on the attempt of the Wallachian government to appropriate the rev
enue of the lands of the monasteries. Since Cuza was in
Moldavia, Giers, who had not previously been informed of
the measure, sought an explanation from the Wallachian
secretary of State, S. Fălcoianu. The latter explained tha
the monasteries had already been put under the obligation

to furnish a contribution to the government in 1844. Although Moldavia had taken its share, Wallachia still refused to be content with the sum then offered. In the Ştirbei administration in 1855 the divan had determined upon the collection of one-fourth of the revenues of the Greek monasteries. This resolution, which was converted into law, was now merely being applied. The tax farmers had been directed to turn their collections into the central treasury to assure that the Wallachian government received its share. Giers protested the illegality of the proceeding and argued that an attempt should have been made first to reach an agreement with the eastern church.[4]

In his report to Gorchakov, Giers pointed out that the quarrel was a revival of an old issue which had now returned with new force. The governments of the Principalities were backed by public opinion for "religious beliefs are unfortunately almost entirely effaced" in the country.[5] Some publications, Giers complained, had even attempted to demonstrate that the hegumens should send to the Holy Places only what revenue remained after the needs of all of the monasteries and local charitable organizations in the Principalities had been met.

Because of the obvious complications which might arise, Giers proposed to step in and mediate the question. In this manner he continued the traditional policy of the Russian government of acting as an arbiter between the governments of the Principalities and the patriarchates. Giers argued strongly that the question should be kept out of the hands of the great powers, including the Porte, who as a body were not sympathetic to the claims of the Orthodox church and would not seek to protect its rights. Giers believed that the church should immediately surrender something in conformity to the engagements they had undertaken previously. Public opinion would be calmed and negotiations towards a definite solution could be undertaken. Delay would be to the detriment of both the church and the Principalities.[6] Giers himself in the spring of 1858 had already warned of the imminence of action against the monasteries. At that time their revenues had doubled, but they had refused to accept suggestions of an equitable settlement.[7]

Giers' immediate remonstrances to the Wallachian government seemed at first to have succeeded. Although

Cuza promised to suspend the measures, he subsequently returned to his earlier decision.[8] Giers, meanwhile, received precise instructions from Gorchakov. On May 5/17 the Russian foreign minister directed Lobanov to:

> Repeat to our agents in the Danubian Principalities the order to oppose energetically the despoiling of monastery property, an intention which is indicated in your despatch No. 58. Prince Cuza should not venture to deviate at all from the decision contained in Protocol XIII of the conferences of Paris. Not only would he put himself in contradiction with solemnly guaranteed rights, but he would incur all the reproof of the powers, who have sanctioned the acts of Paris and of whom the great majority are today disposed to agree to his double election, [an act] which is already not in perfect accord with the thought which has prevailed in the conferences with respect to the reorganization of the Principalities.[9]

In accordance with these definite instructions Giers strongly remonstrated with Cuza when he next saw him on the danger of his acts and reproved him for his vacillating attitude and flagrant violation of Protocol XIII.[10] Cuza protested that he could not fight any longer against the sentiment of the nation on the question of the monasteries, which had not conformed to the stipulations of the original donors. If he constantly thwarted the desires of his compatriots, he would lose their confidence. Moreover, Moldavia had previously received 12,500 ducats a year from the monasteries while Wallachia had gained nothing. Giers protested that the feelings of the nation expressed "by the false doctrines and excitations of the Wallachian press" should not affect the solemn guarantee given to the Greek clergy on its properties; and, continued Giers, "I know very well that it is not on the votes of the men of disorder that Your Highness would seek support, but, in truth, on legality and the observation of the institutions granted to the country." Giers argued that the comparison with Moldavia was not valid since these revenues had been accorded voluntarily whereas Wallachia intended to impose its demands and wished to take as much as a quarter of the revenues of the monasteries.

Before the insistence of the Russian government Cuza in his precarious and uncertain position could do little.

Caught between two fires, he continued his policy of "promising everything and doing nothing." He agreed again to re-
voke the measures provided that the Greek clergy made
some gesture, preferably a voluntary offer similar to that
of 1843 which would save his position at home. In agreeing
to refer this request to Constantinople, Giers, nevertheless, warned Cuza against taking any action detrimental to
the interests of the church which "inspires the pious sollicitude" of the tsar.[11]

The position of the Russian government and of Cuza
now took a settled form. Relying on Protocol XIII Giers
firmly avowed that the Principalities should take action only in agreement with the heads of the Orthodox church; such
an agreement in a definitive form should be negotiated at
once. Giers also urged that the church take an immediate
step toward fulfilling the Rumanian demands for a contribution. In transmitting Cuza's request to Lobanov, Giers
commented that the Holy Fathers would be wise to aid the
government of the Principalities in this time of financial
crisis, particularly in view of the fact that the temporal interests of the church were bound to come up for discussion
in accord with Protocol XIII.[12] Cuza, although promising
not to touch the revenues of the monasteries until a definite
decision had been reached, continuously pressed for a contribution which would provide him with a sufficient motive
for formally revoking the original measure. On their side,
the patriarchs, according to Lobanov, were "disposed to
make at once all the sacrifices possible."[13]

Despite this apparent agreement on the basic issues involved, that is, that the Principalities and the Holy Places
should come to some agreement on the sum that the monasteries should surrender to the state, the entire affair never
progressed beyond this point. In fact, the simple problem
of exactly where negotiations should take place proved impossible to solve in 1859. Until a settlement was reached
in 1866, when Cuza simply appropriated the lands of the
monasteries, no further steps of importance were taken.
Although Cuza did temporarily withdraw the measures
against the monasteries, his actions only led to intermin-
able and involved discussions concerning the technicalities
of the negotiations. On one side, the Holy Fathers were
naturally reluctant to surrender any revenue whatsoever.
Moldavia and Wallachia, in contrast, resented the

exportation of their funds, particularly in view of the impoverished condition of their own country. They also continued to dislike the existence of a foreign administration over so much of their land.

Between the two parties Russia as mediator was in a difficult position. It was quite clear that the governments of the Principalities would go as far as they were allowed toward expropriating the income and lands of the monasteries.[14] As the traditional defender of the eastern church Russia could not allow a serious diminution of the prestige and strength of that institution. The Holy Places depended to a great extent on the income from the Rumanian lands. The issue also was one which would give rise to strong sentiments inside of Russia. Balabin wrote to Giers at this time that the controversy was "unquestionably one of the most important that we have up for consideration and on it will depend to a great extent our relations with the government of the Principalities. No matter from what individual or from what part it comes, enmity in that question will not be forgotten ... "[15]

Nevertheless, Russia could not force a solution on the Principalities to the benefit of the church since, as Giers had previously noted, the matter would not receive great power support. Catholic France, the patron of Rumanian nationalism, would be entirely unsympathetic.[16] The involvement of the western powers would only be to the detriment of the Orthodox church. The Russian government could thus only continue in its role of mediator and recommend moderation, conciliation and a degree of sacrifice to the contending parties. Giers and Lobanov both worked earnestly to impress upon both sides the importance of a quick and fair settlement.

For a time it appeared that the heads of the church would be willing to make concrete concessions. The Patriarch of Jerusalem, for instance, immediately agreed to the contribution of 10,000 ducats which Giers had fixed as the amount which he believed should be paid from the funds dedicated to the Holy Sepulchre. The representatives of Mt. Athos, in contrast, wished more time to reflect.[17] On July 3/15 Giers was able to report that the monasteries were willing to contribute 50,000 ducats to the Wallachian treasury, but with certain conditions attached. Cuza, declaring himself personally satisfied, asked that the hegumens submit the offer to him formally so that he could convoke the council of ministers.[18] Later, however, he showed himself hesitant since he feared the reaction of public opinion should he agree to the conditions. Despite these difficulties Giers at this point was well satisfied with the proceedings.

Meanwhile, conditions had changed in Jassy. Although hitherto the chief complaint of the Orthodox church had been against the Wallachian government, the Moldavian government now proceeded to act and levied 45,000 ducats on the Dedicated Monasteries. The sum, in theory, was the amount which the monasteries owed since the annual payment of 12,500 ducats had been suspended in the Vogorides administration.[19] Giers was extremely angry at this new action: "this conduct, which cannot be condemned enough, shows the capabilities of the irreligious sentiments of the Moldavians and the passionate partiality that they will probably bring into the discussion on the conflict relative to the property of the Greek monasteries."[20]

Giers feared now, since it would be impossible to reach a compromise, that it would be necessary to call in the powers who as a body were inimical toward the eastern church. Under these conditions and considering the men in power in the Principalities, Giers thought that it might be advisable to postpone the implementation of Protocol XIII. In any event it would be better to wait until Cuza had a more conservative ministry, one less dominated by the opinions of the parti exalté. It would be dangerous to allow the latter to negotiate with the Greek clergy since their previous arbitrary acts had betrayed their bias in the matter.[21] The basic difficulty, Giers declared, was that the men in power believed that:

> ... the convention of Paris far from stipulating some rights or immunities in favor of the Greek monasteries in the Principalities accords to the latter, in virtue of their autonomy, the right to administer themselves freely and outside of all foreign interference. The inference that is drawn here from this principle—is that even the existence of the Dedicated Monasteries, subject entirely to the jurisdiction of the country, depends on the will of the Rumanian nation expressed legally by the voice of the elective assembly.[22]

To Giers' arguments on the false interpretation of the August convention, Cuza had previously replied that he was powerless to act as long as his position was not recognized by the powers. In his long report to Lobanov Giers strongly recommended that Cuza be invested only upon his recognition of the convention and of the decisions taken at the conference of Paris and embodied in the protocols.[23]

Despite all of the complexities of the situation, Gorchakov still directed Lobanov to press the clergy to accelerate an agreement in conformity with Protocol XIII. In his discussions in Constantinople Lobanov had few open difficulties with the patriarchs, since, as he reported, they "having a knife at their throats",[24] wished some kind of agreement. They had even accepted Giers' recommendation on the amount to offer. Lobanov continued to press the patriarchs. Giers sought to influence Cuza, the government officials and the hegumens toward conciliation. When Giers saw Cuza again, he urged him to enter into immediate negotiations with the hegumens. Cuza now said that he could not act until the Porte specifically instructed the government to conform to the resolutions of the conference of Paris. If this were done, he would then proceed to form two commissions, one in Moldavia, and one in Wallachia, to handle the matter. Cuza again protested the weakness of his personal position; he preferred to delay until his investiture had been received.[25]

Agreement could not even be reached on the basic question of where the negotiations should be held and who should participate in the discussions. The patriarchs of Jerusalem and Alexandria wished the negotiations to take place in Constantinople when Cuza arrived there for the investiture.[26] Reports circulated that the patriarchs might even go to Rumania. Giers and Lobanov both opposed either of these alternatives. They agreed that the negotiations should be held in Bucharest by plenipotentiaries who would be chosen from the moderates on both sides. Thus, although the term allowed by the conference of Paris for the settlement of the question had been extended at the request of the Russian government, the matter dragged. Lobanov reported that: "this question of the monastery property rightly preoccupies our ministry which sees with regret the covetousness of the Moldo-Wallachian government and its resolutely hostile attitude toward the Orthodox

clergy." Gorchakov himself had instructed Lobanov to recommend to Giers "to be very explicit and firm toward the
Moldo-Wallachian administration and to make it understand
how much the encroachments attempted against the rights
of the church are of a nature to weaken and to modify the
benevolence" of the tsar.[27]

In November the Porte formally invited Cuza to conform to the decisions of the conference of Paris on the Dedicated Monasteries.[28] A. Golescu, the chief of the Depart-
ment of Religion, assured Giers that the Principalities
would bow to the decisions of the powers. Costache Negri,
the agent of the Principalities in Constantinople, had been
instructed to invite the heads of the church to appoint plenipotentiaries to begin discussions. Again the question of
where the negotiations should be held arose. Giers learned
from the hegumens that the patriarchs definitely wished to
negotiate personally at Constantinople and that the Porte
supported them. Although Giers recognized that such an
arrangement would be to the benefit of the church, he
warned that the Principalities would refuse and that they
would be supported by the majority of the powers.[29]

The constitution drawn up by the central commission
followed the radical form of the entire document in its treatment of the monasteries. Here the extreme solution of the
problem was adhered to. The Rumanian church was to remain united to the oecumenical church in all that concerned
dogma, but was to remain independent of foreign authority
in spiritual, canonical and disciplinary matters. Contrary
to Protocol XIII the constitution took out of the hands of the
Greek clergy the right to administer their property in the
Principalities. Needless to say, the church welcomed
Cuza's dissolution of the chambers and the central commission in December.[30]

By the end of the year, therefore, despite the diligent
efforts of Giers and Lobanov, no steps had been taken toward the practical solution of the problem. Neither Cuza
nor the church were eager to make sacrifices; each apparently believed that time was on its side. Russia as mediator was in an unenviable position. Although sympathetic
to the church, she could not afford to alienate or embarrass the government of the Principalities to an extent that
the other powers would be called in. If, however, she allowed the rights of the church to be diminished too far, her

position as the protector of the eastern church would be
damaged and repercussions would be felt at home.

In strong contrast to his position on the question of the
Dedicated Monasteries, Giers' attitude on the second conflict, that over consular jurisdiction, showed at least a tac-
it sympathy with the claims of the Principalities. Consular
jurisdiction in Moldavia and Wallachia rested on rights
gained by the great powers in the capitulations and the treaties existing between the European powers and the Porte.[31]
Rights of extra-territoriality had originally been sought in
the Rumanian lands, as elsewhere in the Ottoman Empire,
in order that Christian Europeans would not be subject to
Moslem courts. Justification for the continuation of such a
policy in a country which was itself Christian and autonomous was difficult to find, but the powers were loath to
surrender rights previously gained, particularly since the
courts of the Principalities were notoriously bad. The Rumanians themselves were extremely sensitive about the
matter of consular jurisdiction since its existence reflected
discreditably on their government and judicial system.
Moreover, in the past consular privileges had been extended and abused by foreigners resident in the Principalities.

In the Règlement organique the Russians had already
tried to place a limitation on foreign jurisdiction. For instance, it had been decided that in civil processes where
one of the parties was a native, the local courts should decide the case; that foreigners engaged in commerce should
submit to all of the regulations and payments required of
natives; and that an exact list of foreigners resident in the
country be maintained and their exact status verified. The
powers were also to abolish any special agencies set up to
protect their citizens. According to Giers' report, only
Russia had observed these rules, and, consequently, the
Russian consulates had fewer conflicts over jurisdiction
than any other country.

The principal difficulties in the question arose after
Cuza was elected when there was general agitation to be
rid of all foreign control, in particular of the obligations
imposed upon the Principalities by the agreements between
the Porte and the powers. Relations between the local authorities and the consulates became increasingly difficult
although many of the foreign representatives hesitated to

press their claims in fear that it might cause further difficulties for the already troubled regime of Cuza. An open
quarrel, however, broke out in Jassy when the government
attempted to apply a new direct tax to foreigners as well as
to natives.[32] This action, put into effect by direct decree,
was in violation of previous agreements and of the convention
which required that no tax be assessed without the approval
of the assemblies. Cuza explained to Giers that he could
not submit the measure to the assembly because of the opposition which that body had shown to his government. He
had to act through administrative measures of a provisional character. Giers replied that this "appeared very irreg-
ular and that, in my opinion, it could create for him great
difficulties in Moldavia."

Although at this meeting, held on July 3/15, Cuza
promised that the measure would be revoked, the question,
as well as that of the Dedicated Monasteries, remained unsettled. Throughout the negotiations, which involved all of
the powers, Giers and Lobanov showed real sympathy for
the Rumanian objections. Moreover, since the principal
sufferer was Austria, the Russians had little interest in associating themselves with protests to protect an arrangement which in the last analysis was chiefly to the benefit of
the Austrian nationals resident in the Principalities. Russia, as Giers wrote to Gorchakov, had constantly fought
"the system of absorption practised abusively in these
lands by Austria by means of its consular jurisdiction
which extends already over a population of more than
100,000 men." When Popov joined in a collective démarche
in Jassy, Lobanov declared that he had exceeded his instructions.[33]

As a solution to the controversy Giers believed that an
entirely new arrangement should be made. He admitted
that it might be necessary that the agreement be made between the powers and the Porte, although he preferred that
it be restricted to those signatory to the August convention.[34] In agreement with the other consuls, Giers emphasized the importance of maintaining some form of consular
jurisdiction because of the condition of the Moldavian and
Wallachian courts. In the immediate disputes he preferred
that Russia not associate herself in action with other powers, but only protest when the rights of a Russian citizen
were involved. Giers also pointed out that concessions in

the matter would cause Russia relatively little inconven-
ience since only a few of her nationals were engaged in
commerce, industry or the professions. Russians were
chiefly involved in affairs relating to landed property and,
according to the capitulations, it was precisely in "disputes
relative to real estate" that consuls could not interfere.
Giers thus recommended that if a new agreement were
made, it might be wise if Russia made large concessions
elsewhere and reserved the right to make special representations to the local authorities if disagreements arose in
this category.

Throughout 1859 Giers was engaged in protracted discussions on other comparatively minor matters. Two of
these, the arranging of a telegraphic convention between
Russia and the Porte[35] and the more involved question of
what the Principalities owed Russia, and vice versa, in
connection with the war and occupations of the previous ten
years,[36] occasioned much diplomatic correspondence but
led to no serious disputes. A third, relating to the Bessa-
rabians who wished to migrate to Russia, was a matter of
considerable discussion. When southern Bessarabia was
assigned to Moldavia in 1856, a three year period was allowed in which those who wished could migrate to Russia.
Serious impediments, however, were placed in the way of
those who wished to dispose of their property before leaving.[37] On Giers' representations Cuza promised to send a
commission to investigate reported abuses by the local authorities.[38] Giers himself was not sympathetic to the encouragement of emigration for very practical reasons. It
would be difficult for the emigrants to settle inside of Russia where land was scarce and prices were rising. If these
same people stayed in Moldavia, Russia would have loyal
adherents in the border regions and their influence would
counteract the latinization of the Principalities.[39]

Thus in the first year of Cuza's administration, the
record of the Russian government in influencing or control-
ling the hospodar was not very impressive. In the one matter of real concern to Russia, the Dedicated Monasteries,
Cuza through one excuse or another, had managed to avoid
committing himself and had succeeded in postponing the
solution of the question. The policy of "promising everything and doing nothing" was once again successful in maintaining the independence of action of the two administration

against foreign pressure. Cuza's constant vacillation was all the more difficult for Giers to handle since Russia could not resort to strong measures particularly when dealing with the religious question in the Principalities. Certainly, the entire controversy demonstrated to the Russian government that the Principalities, united under a single executive, were not going to be easily influenced into following the paths of political development favored in St. Petersburg.

Notes

1. For the problem of the Dedicated Monasteries see Emerit, pp. 167-174; Filitti, pp. 115-120; Iorga, Geschichte des Rumänischen Volkes, pp. 318-322; Riker, pp. 354-358; Seton-Watson, pp. 306-308 and Xenopol, Istoria Românilor, XIII, pp. 176-199. Also "Correspondence from Jassy to the 'Times'". August 16/28, 1857 in Acte și documente, V, pp. 532-534.

2. For an attack on the manner in which the eastern church administered the Dedicated Monasteries see Grégoire Bengesco, Memorandum sur les églises, les monastères, les biens conventuels et spécialement sur les monastères dédiés de la Principauté de Valachie (Bucharest, 1858). The author argues, and presents supporting documents, that the original donors had put the lands under the protection of the Holy Places because at that time the church offered the best guarantee for the carrying out of their desire to maintain public institutions in the Principalities. They had in no way intended to alienate from their country a large proportion of its territory.

3. Riker, p. 357.

4. Giers to Lobanov, No. 30, Bucharest, April 26/ May 8; Giers to Popov, No. 32, Bucharest, May 2/14.

5. Giers to Gorchakov, No. 24, Bucharest, May 2/14.

6. Ibid.; Giers to Lobanov, No. 33, Bucharest, May 9/21.

7. Giers to Butenev, No. 3, n.p., May 11/23, 1858; Giers to Butenev, No. 4, n.p., May 25/ June 6, 1858.

8. Popov to Giers, private letter, Jassy, May 8/20, 1859. Popov believed that the Greek hegumens were really obligated to pay 12,000 ducats to the Moldavian

government. Giers to Gorchakov, No. 29, Bucharest, May 30/ June 11.

9. Giers to Popov, No. 38, Bucharest, May 30/ June 11.

10. Giers to Gorchakov, No. 31, Bucharest, June 5/17

11. Ibid.

12. Giers to Lobanov, No. 39, Bucharest, June 7/19.

13. Lobanov also commented: "What distresses me th most is the latinizing tendency which is seeing light more and more in the Principalities. I cannot recommend to you enough the affair of the monastery property." Lobanov to Giers, private letter, Buyukdere, June 8/20.

14. Cuza's personal attitude toward the matter was apparent in his letter of April 13/25 to Alecsandri. There he wrote that he had decided to raise money for his military preparations by a national subscription rather than a foreign loan because the latter would have to be guaranteed by the monastic lands "which represent a third of our landed property and from which, sooner or later, the country will dispossess the Greek monks." Because of the difficulties which this move would cause with Russia, Cuza did not believe that the time had yet come to seek a foreign loan. Cuza to Alecsandri, Bucharest, April 13/25. Bossy, Agenţia diplomatică a României în Paris, p. 167.

15. Balabin to Giers, private letter, Vienna, (date illegible), 1859.

16. The French, however, supported the Russian attempt at mediation. Lobanov wrote that Thouvenel had told him that "he had written to Béclard to tell him that he approved without any reserve all that we had done in the affair of the monastery property, and to engage him to give you his most loyal and zealous assistance." Lobanov to Giers, private letter, Buyukdere, August 17/29.

17. Lobanov to Giers, private letter, Buyukdere, June 22/ July 4.

18. Giers to Gorchakov, No. 38, Bucharest, July 3/15

19. Giers to Gorchakov, No. 35, confidential, Bucharest, June 27/ July 9; Giers to Popov, No. 45, Bucharest, June 27/ July 9.

20. Giers to Gorchakov, No. 40, Bucharest, July 11/23. Popov continued to argue in favor of the actions of the Moldavian government. He believed that the sum demanded of the monasteries was "very reasonable." The hegumens themselves had told Popov that this amount would be the least that they would have to pay after an agreement had been reached. Popov to Giers, private letter, July 3/15.

21. Giers to Gorchakov, No. 47, August 7/19.

22. Giers to Lobanov, No. 60, Bucharest, August 15/27.

23. Ibid.

24. Lobanov to Giers, private letter, Buyukdere, August 17/29.

25. Giers to Gorchakov, No. 55, Bucharest, September 4/16.

26. Lobanov to Giers, private letter, Buyukdere, September 14/26.

27. Lobanov to Giers, private letter, Buyukdere, September 28/ October 10.

28. Giers to Gorchakov, No. 65, Bucharest, November 6/18. Giers supported the intervention of the Porte to protect the rights of the monasteries in Wallachia. Giers to Gorchakov, No. 52, Bucharest, August 22/ September 3.

29. Giers to Gorchakov, No. 66, Bucharest, November 14/26.

30. Lobanov to Giers, private letter, Pera, November 23/ December 5.

31. "Report on Consular Jurisdiction in the Principalities" in Giers to Gorchakov, No. 74, Bucharest, December 12/24.

32. Giers to Gorchakov, No. 36, Bucharest, July 3/15. See also Riker, pp. 232-234.

33. In contrast to Giers Place reacted violently. Although Giers in his reports paid relatively little attention to the question, Place devoted much space to a denunciation of Cuza and the Moldavian government. (See documents nos. 2737, 2738, 2741, 2742, 2743, 2744, 2746 in Acte și documente, IX). Place's strongest statement is

contained in his despatch of June 30/ July 12: "Ingratitude
is decidedly the distinctive characteristic of these people
who appear in a hurry to return in bad dealings with the
French residents the good that the Emperor's government has
done them. Without a doubt the former regime of the Principalities was filled with abuses. However, those who are
called the large boyars were at times accessible to reason
and justice. But the new men, recently arrived in power
and who have risen from the gutter thanks only to the education which has been given them at our schools, at the expense of these same boyars, show an incapacity which is
comparable only to their feelings of hate against all those
from whom they have received benefits." Place to Walewski, Jassy, June 30/ July 12. Acte și documente, IX, p.
356.

34. Giers' attitude on the consular question is contained
in the despatches already noted (Nos. 36 and 74 to Gorchakov) and in Giers to Gorchakov, No. 64, Bucharest, October 23/ November 5. Gorchakov also preferred that the
question be resolved by a general agreement between the
powers who had consular rights in the Principalities and
who were signatories of the August convention. Gorchakov
to Giers, No. 503, November 9/21, 1859. Russian archives.

35. On the telegraphic convention see in particular:
Giers to Popov, No. 22, (Bucharest), April 10/22; Giers to
Lobanov, No. 31, Bucharest, April 27/ May 9; Giers to
Gorchakov, No. 46, Bucharest, July 31/ August 12; Giers
to Gorchakov, No. 51, Bucharest, August 22/ September 3;
Giers to Gorchakov, No. 53, (Bucharest), August 28/ Sep-
tember 9; Giers to Gorchakov, No. 72, Bucharest, Decem-
ber 4/16.

36. Giers to Tolstoi, No. 21, Bucharest, April 4/16.

37. Giers to Gorchakov, No. 26, Bucharest, May 16/
28.

38. Giers to Gorchakov, No. 33, Bucharest, June 19/
July 1; Giers to Gorchakov, No. 49, Bucharest, August 14/
26.

39. Giers to Gorchakov, No. 50, Bucharest, August
22/ September 3.

Chapter VII

CONCLUSION: THE LEGISLATIVE AND ADMINISTRATIVE UNION OF THE PRINCIPALITIES

Certainly, it cannot be said that the pattern of political development in the Principalities by the end of 1859 conformed to Russian desires or interests. Under the leadership of Cuza, the combined administrations of Wallachia and Moldavia had shown not only great independence before Russian prompting, but had also failed to establish true internal order and stability or to show respect for their international obligations. Henceforth, the documentation from Russian sources becomes increasingly meager, but it is apparent from the despatches of the agents of the other powers that the Russian government was becoming more dissatisfied with the course of events in the Principalities and less reluctant to combat openly activities supported by France in the area.

It has already been emphasized how the Russian entente with France gave at least indirect Russian sanction to the European movements favored by Napoleon III which in their basic structure were revolutionary in the Russian definition. In 1859 and 1860 the unification of Italy was for all practical purposes accomplished. The second phase with the prominence of Garibaldi and the overthrow of an established monarchy in the Kingdom of Naples had underlined the revolutionary significance of the national unification movements. The defeat of Austria, the archfoe of nationalism in central Europe, had given added hope to the submerged nationalities of the Ottoman Empire and Russia as well as the Danubian empire. After the establishment of the Kingdom of Italy it was immediately apparent that a bond of sympathy and support united that nation with the national movements in central and southeastern Europe, in particular, with the Principalities who had not yet achieved effective national unification, and further with the Hungarian and Polish revolutionary leaders. It was natural for the conservative Russian observer to feel himself menaced by the spectre of a great revolutionary conspiracy embracing the governments of Italy and the Principalities, the Polish and Hungarian revolutionaries, and even the states of Serbia, Montenegro and Greece.[1] All of these elements were in revolt either against the political structure of the governments under which they lived or against the territorial organization of Europe. The achievement of their aims would mean the destruction or severe curtailment of the Austrian, Russian and Ottoman empires.

It has also been mentioned that in the years covered by this study the commissions entrusted with the land reform question in Russia were completing their tasks. Throughout Russia uncertainty and anxiety over the consequences of peasant emancipation pervaded the country.[2] Both the Russian government and the landowners as a class were under increasing financial pressure. The fear of a radical solution to the social questions and of uprisings within Russia were widespread. The connections between the Russian radical elements and the revolutionary leaders in central and southeastern Europe were known and were watched for their possible effects on Russian internal conditions. In the winter of 1862/1863 Gorchakov wrote to Giers:

> For goodness sake, do not treat that question with too much indifference. Even if the material nucleus in the Principalities is not tremendous, the relations which your revolutionaries seek to establish with our malcontents of the empire or of the kingdom [of Poland] should be followed with unceasing solicitude. It could happen that the Principalities would furnish a thread that would end in important discoveries in the interior of the empire or of the kingdom. Thus you will follow and you will deal with that question without respite or fatigue under all its forms.[3]

Giers' attitude toward the liberals, whom he designated by terms such as the parti exalté and les rouges, has already been discussed, and it must be remembered that the Russian consul was a moderate. Those with more rightist leanings were even more disturbed by the events in the Principalities and their connection with the revolutionary movements in Europe.

The relations between the Principalities and Italy were so close that the Russian government made it a matter of diplomatic correspondence.[4] Russia was particularly concerned over reports that Rumanian students were to be sent to Italian universities and that some of Cuza's officers were to train in the Italian army. Gorchakov instructed Giers to protest against this latter measure and to advise Cuza that Rumanian policy should remain independent, that it should not be revolutionary, and that it should not be concerned with the Rumanians still under Austrian rule.[5] The entire question of the relations between Italy, the Principalities and Hungary exploded into a real crisis in December 1860 when two Sardinian ships unloaded arms at Galatz destined for Hungary. The resultant crisis, which has been discussed at length elsewhere,[6] brought to the fore the dangerous consequences possible from the cooperation of the governments of the new national states.

Meanwhile, Cuza continued to be unable to form in either Principality a government capable of administering the state effectively. Forced into repeated changes of ministers the hospodar found that he lacked a sufficient number of competent leaders on whom he could depend for efficient administration and that the two major political groups were unable to stifle factional quarrels in the interest of their country. It was also obvious to all that the complicated mechanism of government with the two assemblies, the two ministries and the central commission was entirely too cumbersome to manage. Unable to conduct the internal affairs of the Principalities under such a system, Cuza found himself forced by all parties into further moves toward union and further actions in the national interest. This development was regarded with great disfavor in St. Petersburg. Gorchakov complained to Bismarck, who was the Prussian representative in Russia at this time, that "Cuza is posing as the Romulus of the Rumanians, and he speaks in the style of the bulletins of the first Napoleon; Cavour must have blown into that balloon in order to inflate it to this point; those people there forget altogether what they are and from where they came ... "[7] Russian dislike of the internal events in the Principalities and of the direction of French policy in the region led the Russian government to adopt a position in the next crisis in the Principalities which, although not openly hostile, was inimical to the development of the Rumanian nation.

In 1860 Cuza was faced with the necessity of solving three major internal problems which were inseparably interconnected: administrative reform, agrarian reform and a change in the electoral law. Discussions on rural affairs held during the year clearly showed that as long as the conservatives dominated the legislatures, because of the franchise system, agrarian reform in the true sense would be impossible. The conservatives for their part remained, quite understandably, adamant on both the agrarian and electoral questions. It was recognized that until real union were achieved, Cuza would be unable to make any advances in dealing with these problems. Moreover, the fight for legislative and administrative union was an issue on which all parties could unite. The left had consistently supported any measures which would further the Rumanian national cause; the right hoped that Cuza would either so compromise himself that he would be forced out of office or that the controversy would result in the establishment of a foreign prince in the country.[8] The hospodar, because of his preference for ministries of moderates and liberals and because of his apparent determination to institute agrarian reform, had won the animosity of the conservatives who now, as previously, continued to base their political orientation on the attitude of each succeeding administration to the land question.

Cuza, therefore, directed his energies toward securing the administrative and legislative union of the Principalities. He wisely centered his attention on the suzerain power.[9] Ably assisted by the representative of the Principalities at Constantinople, Costache Negri, Cuza by the spring of 1861 was able to persuade the Porte to agree to the establishment of a single ministry and assembly and the abolition of the central commission. This change, however, was to last only for the lifetime of Cuza.[10] The Porte also advised the hospodar to submit a plan of electoral reform to the powers for consideration. With the acceptance by the Porte of the real unification of the

Principalities, the question still remained of the manner in which the guarantor states should signify their approval or rejection of the plan. France and Britain, fearing a conference because of the uncertain status of Victor Emmanuel as King of Italy, wanted the powers individually to submit their opinions to the Porte. Weakened by the Italian war, even Austria did not protest. The opposition at first came exclusively from Gorchakov who argued that it would be impossible to limit unification to Cuza's reign and that the final result would be the establishment of a foreign dynasty in Bucharest and the lasting unification of the Principalities. The Russian government had always opposed a foreign prince since it was obvious that he would come from a western or central European family and would in all probability be a Catholic. Russian influence in the country would consequently be even further diminished. Gorchakov believed that it would be preferable to reform the existing structure rather than to change the previous agreements.[11] In any case, he thought that these could not be modified without the summoning of an international conference, which he wished held in Paris rather than in Constantinople.[12]

The majority of the foreign representatives agreed with Bismarck's analysis of the Russian reaction. The Prussian ambassador believed that the Russians were against the proposal and were trying to complicate the entire affair. They were unwilling to take a firm stand against France and Rumanian unification, but they hoped that a conference would refuse to sanction the action.[13] The opinion was also expressed that the Russian government resented the French assumption that Russia would follow the lead of Paris in Rumanian affairs under all circumstances. Undoubtedly, the Russian government was strongly unfavorable toward the new developments, but Gorchakov hesitated to make the matter the occasion for a major breach with France. In the subsequent months he contented himself with throwing up obstacles to union wherever possible and in protracting the discussions as much as possible.

The entire question became a matter of much diplomatic correspondence in June and July of 1861. When it became apparent that he would receive no support from other powers, Gorchakov abandoned his insistence on a conference and shifted his attack to other grounds. He now argued that the electoral law should be discussed first; he even signified his approval of a suggestion that union be granted for only three years and then discussed again. Although he received a measure of support from Austria and the Porte, Gorchakov was finally forced to capitulate and accept real union. The final discussions centered on the question of the enforcement of the provision that the union was only to last for the lifetime of Cuza. Here Russia joined the powers in opposing granting the Porte an unlimited right of intervention. Finally the Protocol of 1859 was reaffirmed and it was generally recognized that the union was permanent. With the issuance of the firman on the new arrangement, Cuza could with justice proclaim, "Rumanians, union is accomplished. The Rumanian nationality is founded! ... Long live Rumania."[14]

The accomplishment of the legislative and administrative union of the Principalities was the last problem connected with that nation which France and Russia dealt with under the entente established in 1856. The Russian reaction to the French proposals throughout the discussions had shown not only how far Russian interests were separate from the French in the Principalities, but also the increasing reluctance with which Gorchakov followed the French lead in Rumanian affairs. Gorchakov did not hesitate to disclose his disgust and distaste with the French treatment of his proposals and he disliked the facility with which the Principalities had been able to dispense with the limitations which the powers had imposed on them. "What will become of the previous engagements of the powers?", he complained. "These are dangerous theories to which Russia and Austria as adjacent states of the Principalities cannot associate themselves."[15]

Gorchakov's policy, that is, the maintenance of an entente with France designed to offset British and Austrian opposition in the Balkans and the Near East, to split the Crimean coalition and at the same time to preserve Russia from isolation, and, if possible, to break the offending clauses of the Treaty of Paris, had much to be said in its favor. From 1856 to 1863 Russia did gain a breathing space; at the same time she made important advances in Asia without the necessity of being concerned with an immediate military problem in the west. The failure of the policy lay precisely in those contradictions in aim and purpose between Russia and France which we have seen operate in Rumanian affairs. The French policy, pursued aggressively, of the national organization of Europe was not consistent with Russian interests or with the convictions of the politically significant groups in Russia, none of whom held any sympathies toward liberalism or nationalism as guiding motives in Russian foreign policy. The element that was rising in importance in the determination of foreign policy was conservative and panslav.[16] Gorchakov was repeatedly forced to justify his policy in the name of Russian nationalism and Russian national interests. Yet obviously the establishment of a Kingdom of Italy, with absolutely no compensation to Russia, was not to Russia's benefit, particularly since the path to union was strewn with broken international agreements and with revolutionary acts. The unification of Rumania under liberal leadership was a similar matter. The Russo-French friendship lasted through the union of Moldavia and Wallachia and through the unification of Italy, but it broke on the Polish question, a matter far closer to Russia and one which involved the integrity of her empire.

Russian disappointment with France on her attitude toward the unrest and disquiet in Poland was apparent throughout 1861.[17] Although the governments remained on friendly terms, the Russians reproached the French with failing to act in conformity with their declarations. When open revolt broke out in Poland in January 1863, the Russian entente with France finally came to an end. It is difficult to see how Gorchakov could not have foreseen that in strengthening the French position in Europe and in allowing her sponsorship of Rumanian and Italian nationalism, the very success of these movements would inspire similar agitation in Russian controlled provinces, particularly in Catholic and western-oriented Poland. Although the Russian government had viewed with equanimity the reduction of Austrian power in Italy and had favored the overthrow of Ottoman rule in the Balkans, it could not accept similar movements to its own detriment. The Polish revolt thus forced a realignment in Russian foreign relations; Russia needed a substitute for France to avoid the situation in which she had found herself in the Crimean war.

With the dropping of France the logical step for

Russian policy would have been an attempt at the recreation of the former conservative alliance. Much of Gorchakov's animosity toward Austria had abated by this time. In 1861, when angry with France over the Principalities, he had declared on the subject of Russian relations with Austria: "Our rapprochement is at present only a thread, but that thread can become a rope."[18] In 1863 he made the following comment:

> I hope very much ... that in Berlin they do not believe any more that my former hatred against Austria still lasts. Today I render full justice to the loyalty of the court of Vienna and I wish sincerely to go along with her. I am fair-minded, but I am a Russian before all. I recognize only the interests of Russia. I do not love anyone and I do not hate anyone. If the interests of Russia required it, I would even make a pact with the devil and without hesitation I would throw myself into his arms.[19]

And this, in fact, is exactly what he did. The major consequence of the Polish revolt for Europe was the subsequent drawing together of Prussia and Russia. On the basis of the Russian friendship and by skilful diplomatic manoeuvering Bismarck was able to secure German unification and establish German hegemony on the continent. It is a poor comment on Gorchakov's diplomatic ability and foresight that to save Russia from the dangers of Polish nationalism and diplomatic isolation, he was henceforth to acquiesce to a far greater danger to his country in the fulfillment of Prussian and German national aims.

With the end of her tie with France, Russia lost influence in the Principalities. The chief Russian interest, the fate of the Dedicated Monasteries, had, as we have seen, remained unsettled in 1859. At that time France had supported the Russian position. Negotiations between the Principalities and the heads of the church dragged on inconclusively through the next years until in 1864 Cuza secularized the monastic lands and offered in return an indemnity.[20] Since Cuza had again violated an international understanding, the powers once more became involved in Rumanian affairs. France backed the Principalities;[21] Britain took the role of the principal opposing power. Although Russia continued to try to obtain a settlement favorable to the

eastern church, or at least to save something from the disaster to Orthodox interests, she could do nothing but protest. Bismarck, who consistently maintained that Prussia
had no interest in Rumania, refused to embroil his country
with France on the question. Since no power would use
force against Cuza or allow another state to undertake the
task, the government of Rumania in the end acquired title
to the vast lands of the monasteries without the necessity
of paying anything at all.

By 1862 the principal steps toward the foundation of the
modern Rumanian state had been accomplished. In 1866
Cuza was expelled and a foreign prince, Charles of Hohenzollern—Sigmaringen, was put on the throne, an act which
signified the final fulfillment of the program of the unionists
after 1856. In 1878 Rumania received full independence
from the Ottoman Empire. In the achievement of national
unification, Rumania was indebted to Russia only in a negative sense. Russian policy from 1858 to 1863 toward the
Rumanian national movement had been, as we have seen,
that of reluctant acquiescence to events precipitated on Rumanian initiative and subsequently backed by France. Russian support had been given to the French position in Rumanian affairs with the hope of receiving in return benefits for
Russia's eastern endeavors, not with the intention of aiding
the Rumanian national movement as such. In the final accounting, Russia lost the game; she gained no concrete concessions from the French alignment and the creation of a
Rumanian state was to the detriment of her interests.
Thereafter, Rumania remained linked to the west; she
strengthened ties with the Habsburg Monarchy and Germany
and remained in sympathy close to her "Latin" brother
states, France and Italy. The liberal influence in Rumanian politics had assured that the direction of the national
movement would be toward the west and antipathetic to Russian autocracy. The common Orthodox religion had failed
to act as a lasting bond.

The unification of Moldavia and Wallachia, unlike that
of Italy or later of Germany, was accomplished completely
through diplomacy and the ballot box and was unaccompa-
nied by bloodshed of any sort. Cuza became hospodar of
both provinces through a legal election, legally carried out;
the administrative and legislative union was brought about
through international action on the initiative of the suzerain

power. In a sense the relative smoothness with which Rumanian unification was achieved was occasioned by the timing of the events which transpired. It is difficult to imagine such ease of accomplishment either before or after this period. A child of a marriage of convenience between Russia and France, Rumania was a matter of prime concern to neither of the powers. France was quite willing to consider the possibility of giving the Principalities to Austria in return for Lombardy and Venetia; Russia was far more concerned with the fate of the Dedicated Monasteries, which involved the Russian position in the entire Orthodox world, than with any individual issue in Rumanian politics alone. Rumanian was united under the shadow of far more dramatic events in Italy and retained her unity because of the precarious balance between the great powers.

In conclusion, a final word must be said concerning the two chief figures in our account— Giers and Cuza. Of the two Giers achieved the least success in attaining the objective of his policy which was, of course, to assure stable governments in the Principalities which would take no further moves toward union and to establish Russian influence firmly in Jassy and Bucharest. The main reason for his failure lay, however, not in his own activities or in his personal failings, but in the contradictory nature of the policy which he was called upon to pursue. Instructed to cooperate with France, who stood in Rumanian eyes for union and the rule of the liberal party, he could not openly combat either the unionists or those who stood for the continued latinization of the Principalities. As long as Russia was cooperating with France, the pursuit of the real Russian national interests in the area would be severely curtailed. Since the Russian government did not want a crisis in the east, Giers could also not use force or the threat of force, the ultimate weapon in diplomacy, even in the matters of vital concern to Russia such as that of the Dedicated Monasteries.

Giers was also personally unsympathetic to Rumanian nationalism. Unlike Popov who rejoiced in the national victories, Giers could only see the injury done to the section of Rumanian society to which he was most closely associated. Although he apparently did not attempt directly to influence government policy, except towards moderation and order, before the double election, we have seen how

after January 24/ February 5, 1859 he always advised Cuza
to make his appointments from the conservatives. He not
only was unable to impress Cuza in this regard, but also in
other matters, such as the establishment of the central
commission, the affair of the Dedicated Monasteries, the
establishment of the military camp near Ploeşti and even
the problem of the Bessarabian emigrants. Yet here again
Giers cannot be judged too harshly for his failures. Cuza
and the Rumanian unionists were bound to resist Russian
pressure. They recognized that Russia had no real interest in a strong Rumania; as an adjacent state she would always be a menace to Rumanian independence. Even the
conservatives, despite their anxieties over the agrarian
question, never became Russian tools. No individual agent,
however clever, would have been able to offset the basic
conditions of the time.

Giers' period in office in Bucharest was, therefore,
just another step in a long and successful career. Although
it was a period of personal hardship and anxiety for himself and his family, he performed his duties with care and,
certainly, to the satisfaction of his superiors. He was undoubtedly delighted when his duties in Bucharest came to an
end and his long association with the Principalities appears
to have left him with no lasting affection for the country or
particularly pleasant memories.

In contrast, Cuza served his nation with remarkable
success in the first year of his sudden elevation to power.
It must be repeated that Cuza was not ambitious in the true
sense of the term. He accepted his position as a temporary substitute for a foreign prince. His people had never
been willing to recognize supreme authority in one of their
fellow countrymen. When it is considered that he could not
even count on the unstinted support of the liberal party, it
must be recognized that he played an able game of balanc-
ing the opposing political forces in the Principalities.
Moreover, he did gain the acquiescence of the powers for
his double election. Later he achieved the legislative and
administrative union of the Principalities without precipitat-
ing an international crisis. His record in foreign policy
was thus excellent. He can, of course, be criticized for
his failure to provide leadership within the country or to
formulate and carry through a set domestic program at
this time. However, it is to be doubted whether he could

have done more than he did even if he had been so inclined.
Later he was able to put through positive measures only by
using dictatorial procedures. In 1859, before he had received the consent of the powers to his double election, he
certainly could not have openly violated the constitutional
provisions of the country to such a flagrant extent.

Cuza's success in resisting Russian influence was, as
we have seen, also remarkable. He was able to withstand
Russian pressure in almost all matters. He did this by
avoiding a direct challenge on any issue—by promising everything and doing nothing. Although his methods left much
to be desired in political ethics, these virtues in central
and southeastern Europe were always a luxury enjoyed by
only the strong nations. He was certainly wise in putting
his trust in France. Although that nation always subordi-
nated Rumanian interests to those of Italy, France offered
no direct threat to Rumanian freedom. In contrast to Russia, France was not only far away, but her policy could only benefit from the establishment of a strong Danubian state
between Russia and the Habsburg Monarchy. If Rumania
were to be a "little France", that signified only a conquest
of French culture and civilization; if Rumania became a
"little Russia", she would be reduced to another Poland.

Therefore, in the final analysis, with the establishment
on the Danube and adjacent to her territory of a potentially
hostile nation, Russia had indeed suffered a diplomatic defeat. In the preceding decades she had either directly controlled the territory or it was in the safe hands of a weak
authority. Russia in either case had a free passage to Constantinople. Moreover, formerly, in the boyar class and in
the Orthodox religious establishments Russia had adherents
within the country on whom she could count in time of war.
The situation had now radically changed. Rumania alone
was, of course, not a danger to Russia, but in alliance with
a hostile central European power she could menace the Russian position in the Near East and threaten the Ukraine. In
Bessarabia Russia and Rumania had a disputed territory
whose fate was never determined to the satisfaction of both
parties but which remained a constant dividing issue between them. Henceforth, Russia in the 1860s and 1870s
turned more toward the Balkan Slavs to find support for her
eastern policy. In the next twenty years she was to attempt
with an equal lack of success, to win the Bulgarian people

into her camp and to make of an autonomous and strong Bulgaria a bridge to Constantinople.

Notes

1. See Schlözer, Petersburger Briefe, p. 182; Bismarck to Schleinitz, (St. Petersburg), December 28/ January 9, 1861. Bismarck: Die gesammelten Werke, edited by H. von Petersdorff, (Berlin, 1924-1930), III, pp 160-162; A.P.P., II², fn. 2 to Doc. 299, p. 38 and fn. 2 to Doc. 312, p. 77. Lobanov commented on the unrest in Poland: "From the impression that I have been able to gather here from certain individuals of the Polish emigration, these disorders should be attributed exclusively to local circumstances and are connected in no manner to some vast plan of conspiracy. What I fear is that they will not be too much impressed at Petersburg and that will throw us into a policy, whose errors we have, alas!, paid for dearly enough." Lobanov to Giers, private letter, Pera, February 27/ March 11, 1861.

2. Lobanov wrote: "There are disorders even in Russia; revolutionary committees are also organized there; constitutions and an overthrow of the dynasty are spoken of ... Where are we going? And with all that we must carry on a foreign policy, we must have influence!" Lobanov to Giers, private letter, Buyukdere, October 9/21, 1861.

3. Gorchakov to Giers, private letter, St. Petersburg, December 29/ January 10, 1862/1863.

4. Schlözer, Petersburger Briefe, p. 180.

5. Bismarck to Schleinitz, (St. Petersburg), November 26/ December 8, 1860. Bismarck: Ges. Werke, III, pp. 142-143.

6. Riker, pp. 274-278.

7. Bismarck to Schleinitz, (St. Petersburg), November 28/ December 10, 1861. Bismarck: Ges. Werke, III, p. 147.

8. St. Pierre to Gruner, n.p., July 12, 1861. A.P.P., II², fn. 2 to Doc. 409, p. 455.

9. See Riker, pp. 288-341. For the reports of the Austrian agents see Bossy, L'Autriche et les Principautés-Unies, pp. 34-58 and the accompanying documents. Some

material relative to this question is presented in: France. Ministère des affaires étrangères, Documents diplomatiques. 1861 (Paris, 1862), pp. 75-89. Appendix IV contains extracts from Lobanov's letters on the question of real union and the Russian objections.

10. Lobanov noted the improvement in the relations between the Porte and the Principalities after Negri's arrival. "I do not know," he wrote, "what the secret is that Cuza has employed to win the good will of the Porte." Lobanov to Giers, private letter, Pera, February 28/ March 11, 1860.

11. See Bismarck to Schleinitz, (St. Petersburg), April 29/ May 11, 1861. Bismarck: Ges. Werke, III, pp. 234-235; Bismarck to Schleinitz, (St. Petersburg), April 29/ May 11, 1861. Ibid., III, pp. 237-238; A.P.P., II², fn. 4 to Doc. 380, p. 337 and fn. 2 to Doc. 409, pp. 454-455.

12. Bismarck to Schleinitz, (St. Petersburg), May 10/ 22, 1861. Bismarck: Ges. Werke, III, p. 249.

13. Bismarck to Schleinitz, (St. Petersburg), May 3/15, 1861. Ibid., III, pp. 243-244; Bismarck to Schleinitz, (St. Petersburg), June 16/28, 1861. Ibid., III, p. 260.

14. Riker, p. 340.

15. Report of Schlözer of August 30/ September 11, 1861. A.P.P., II², fn. 1 to Doc. 409, p. 454.

16. See Michael B. Petrovich, The Emergence of Russian Panslavism, 1856-1870, (New York, 1956), especially pp. 129-153.

17. Schlözer to Sydow, St. Petersburg, September 9/21 1861. A.P.P., II², pp. 454-457; also ibid., fn. 4 to Doc. 409, p. 456. See also Meyendorff's discussion. of the implications of the French entente and the Polish question in Otto Hoetzsch, editor, Peter von Meyendorff: Ein russischer Diplomat an den Höfen von Berlin und Wien, (Berlin and Leipzig, 1923), III, pp. 232-237.

18. Schlözer report of August 31/ September 12, 1861. Ibid., fn. 1 to Doc. 409, p. 454.

19. Redern to Bismarck, St. Petersburg, March 26/ April 7, 1863. A.P.P., III, pp. 451-452.

20. Riker, pp. 430-436.

21. See S. Reinach, "Charles Tissot à Jassy (et à la

Commission des Couvents dédiés); 1863-1866," Revue historique de Sud-Est européen, I, Nos. 7-9, 1924, pp. 205-233.

APPENDICES

I. GORCHAKOV'S INSTRUCTIONS TO GIERS ON THE RUSSIAN POSITION IN THE PRINCIPALITIES.

II. GIERS' REPORT ON THE ELECTION OF CUZA IN WALLACHIA.

III. A REPORT BY LOBANOV ON THE RUSSIAN POSITION IN CONSTANTINOPLE IN THE SUMMER OF 1859.

IV. EXTRACTS FROM THE LETTERS OF LOBANOV TO GIERS ON THE LEGISLATIVE AND ADMINISTRATIVE UNION OF THE PRINCIPALITIES.

APPENDIX I

GORCHAKOV'S INSTRUCTIONS TO GIERS ON THE RUSSIAN
POSITION IN THE PRINCIPALITIES[1]

Le Ministère Impérial vient de m'envoyer les instructions qui
me tracent la ligne de conduite que j'aurai à suivre dans l'exercice
de mes nouvelles fonctions. Ces instructions contiennent un exposé complet de la situation actuelle des Principautés telle qu'elle
a été créée par la guerre d'Orient et déterminée dans les conditions essentielles par la Convention du 7/19 août.

Après avoir rappelé les événements qui ont marqué la dernière crise orientale, et caractérisé l'attitude des différentes
Puissances appelées à concourir à l'oeuvre de paix qui en a posé
le terme, le Prince Gortchacow s'attache à définir les principes
qui doivent servir de base à notre politique dans les Principautés
depuis que nous avons fait l'abandon de nos droits exclusifs dans
ces pays.

Voici en substance ces instructions dont je crois devoir,
Monsieur, vous faire part pour votre gouverne personnelle.

Notre Auguste Maître continue d'étendre sur ces provinces la
même sollicitude bienveillante que Sa Majesté Impériale a vouée
aux autres populations chrétiennes de l'Orient si étroitement
unies à la Russie par la communauté de culte.

Nous ne poursuivons à leur égard aucune vue politique, aucun intérêt particulier. Nous n'y recherchons aucune influence
exclusive, aucune domination.

Mais nous ne pouvons y tolérer aucune prépondérance étran-
gère.

Politiquement nous désirons leur neutralité sous l'égide des
garanties qui les protègent.

Nous y sommes doublement intéressés en qualité de Puissance limitrophe.

En même temps nos sympathies traditionnelles pour ces provinces nous font désirer de maintenir leurs droits acquis, de garantir les privilèges et immunités qu'elles nous doivent et de leur
assurer aujourd'hui sur la base du traité de paix comme nous
l'avons fait autrefois sur celle de nos traités particuliers, toutes
les conditions d'ordre, de prospérité et de liberté compatibles
avec les circonstances actuelles.

Notre but reste donc invariablement le même, nos moyens
d'action ont seuls changé.

Pour avoir à s'exercer en commun ils n'en sont pas aujour-
d'hui moins nettement reconnus et définis; nous avons acquis le
droit de travailler ouvertement à l'accomplissement d'une tâche
que désormais l'Europe partage avec nous; et si dans cette voie
nous rencontrons des obstacles, nous pouvons aussi trouver des
appuis.

Ainsi, tant que durera l'état de choses créé par la dernière
guerre, notre mission dans les Principautés comme dans tout
l'Orient, sera de veiller à la stricte exécution des transactions
qui l'ont constitué, parce qu'en définitive bien qu'issues d'une pen-
sée hostile à notre égard elles consacrent au profit des populations chrétiennes les fruits de nos efforts persévérants, qu'elles
opposent une barrière à des empiètements dangereux, un obstacle
à des complications sérieuses, que leur maintien est le seul gage
de la paix, et que pour être observées par ceux qu'elles gênent
dans leurs tendances, il faut qu'elles soient respectées par ceux
qu'elles protègent dans leurs intérêts et leur sécurité.

Ces considérations nous tracent une double série de devoirs
parallèles également importants.

Les premiers consisteront à prévenir les tentatives de la
Porte et des Puissances qui la conseillent pour étendre les pré-
rogatives du pouvoir suzerain et son intervention dans les affaires intérieures des provinces vassales au delà des limites
posées par la Convention du 7/19 août. Leurs efforts dans ce but
se renouvelleront probablement soit par une interprétation arbi-
traire des termes du nouveau statut organique, soit par une ingé-
rence abusive dans les opérations électorales, les discussions
des assemblées ou l'action des pouvoirs légalement constitués.
Ils doivent être surveillés attentivement et déjoués avec fermeté.

Les seconds consisteront à éclairer l'opinion publique et les
hommes influents dans les deux Principautés sur leurs véritables
intérêts.

Quelque imparfaite que soit l'organisation dont elles ont été
dotée, cette oeuvre telle qu'elle est sortie des mains de la conférence n'en est pas moins désormais la base de leur droit public.

Plus l'enfantement en a été laborieux, plus elles doivent at-
tacher de prix à la maintenir à l'abri de toute atteinte, et à consolider les avantages qu'elle leur offre en travaillant d'un commun
accord à assurer le jeu régulier et le développement normal de
leurs nouvelles institutions.

Ces institutions n'existent encore qu'en théorie. Il s'agit de
les mettre en pratique. Nous devons prévoir bien des déceptions
Les passions seront éveillées, les ambitions excitées; les influences politiques hostiles se mettront à l'oeuvre pour exploiter
ces ferments de discorde; elles trouveront une occasion propice
dans les agitations de l'esprit public lors des élections des assemblées et de celles des hospodars. Des désordres peuvent
éclater et entraîner des interventions qui dans l'état de l'Orient

et de l'Europe provoqueraient des complications dangereuses. Elles compromettraient l'avenir des Principautés en accréditant aux yeux de l'Europe une opinion que l'on s'est déjà efforcé de propager, à savoir: que leur administration indépendante et nationale n'est pas compatible avec l'existence de l'Empire Ottoman.

C'est à prévenir ces dangers que nous devrons nous appliquer en nous addressant à tous les hommes intelligents et bien intentionnés en les groupant autour de nous dans l'intérêt du maintien de l'ordre. Au moment d'entrer dans une nouvelle phase de leur existence, les Moldo-Valaques ne doivent se faire aucune illusion sur les chances qui leur sont offertes, les périls auxquels ils ont échappé, ceux qui les menacent encore, et les appuis sur lesquels ils peuvent compter.

Notre rôle ne doit donc point être stérile et passif. Mais il doit rester dans son activité en dehors de toute intrigue. Ce n'est pas sur de semblables moyens que nous devons fonder notre influence. C'est par la rectitude de sa conduite, par le respect et la confiance qu'elle lui conciliera, que le Consul de Russie, sans pactiser avec aucun parti, doit acquérir l'autorité nécessaire pour faire écouter de salutaires conseils.

Le Cabinet Impérial n'exclut ni ne favorise personne, il n'a ni candidats à produire ni créatures à protéger. Il s'abstient même de sonder le passé. En face d'une situation nouvelle, son appui est assuré d'avance à tous ceux qui apprécient ses intentions tutélaires et disposés à les seconder, se réuniront dans un sentiment de respect pour l'ordre de choses légalement établi dans un but d'ordre, d'améliorations et de progrès dans la conservation.

En suivant dans cet esprit la marche des affaires intérieures des Principautés nous ne devons pas perdre de vue les influences politiques qui viendront à s'y produire du dehors.

Les tendances de la politique autrichienne sont notoires.

Le travail incessant qu'elle a entrepris sur le Danube se manifeste par une activité qui prend toutes les formes et admet toutes les voies. Elle tend à fonder sa domination sur les Principautés par une assimilation politique industrielle et commerciale à laquelle le Cabinet de Vienne travaille sans relâche. Influence politique sur les dépositaires du pouvoir, action mystérieuse sur les partis, appel aux passions, extention abusive de la jurisdiction consulaire, intervention dans toutes les affaires financières, commerciales et industrielles du pays, empiètements administratifs et même territoriaux—tous les moyens lui sont bons. Cette activité pernicieuse nous est particulièrement hostile. Elle exigera de votre part une surveillance assidue.

Malgré la partialité visible du Cabinet de Londres pour la politique actuelle de l'Autriche et de la Porte il est difficile d'admettre que le Gouvernement britannique aille aussi loin dans cette voie peu conforme à ses principes, à ses traditions libérales et aux conditions d'une popularité qu'il a toujours recherchée.

La Prusse n'ayant point d'intérêt direct dans les Principauté a joué dans les dernières négotiations le rôle d'une impartialité bienveillante et conciliatrice qui l'a constamment rapprochée de nos vues. Les liens qui nous unissent au Cabinet de Berlin nous portent à rechercher en toute occasion son concours amical. La rectitude de nos vues ne nous permet pas de douter que nous ne trouvions dans l'influence de leurs agents dans les Principautés des utiles auxiliaires.

Quant à la France, l'entente établie entre cette Puissance et la Russie et consacrée l'année dernière à Stuttgart par un loyal échange d'idées et d'assurances amicales entre les deux Augustes Souverains, a principalement pris corps sur le terrain de l'Orien Elle a pour point de départ la circulaire adressée par les deux Gouvernements à leurs agents en Turquie et qui leur prescrit d'éviter toute lutte d'influence entre eux, surtout dans les questio religieuses et de marcher autant que possible dans les voies d'un complet accord. Elle s'est développée dans les divers incidents qui ont surgi depuis lors et aujourd'hui elle est le gage du mainti de la paix, de la sécurité des populations chrétiennes et de l'influence politique des deux Gouvernements en Orient.

Dans la question spéciale des Principautés, cette entente a surtout contribué à déjouer des tentations rivales et hostiles.

Nous ne saurions donc apporter trop de soin à cultiver avec nos collègues de France des relations amicales en imprimant à notre attitude le caractère d'un intime accord avec eux. Le Prince Gortchacow ne doute pas que les directions dont ils seron munis de leur côté ne nous facilitent cette tâche.

En me donnant ces directions le Prince Gortchacow ajoute qu'à mesure que nos rapports l'éclaireront sur la marche des choses lors des élections et de l'installation des divers pouvoirs qui vont se constituer, il ne manquera pas de vous faire parveni les ordres de Sa Majesté l'Empereur sur toutes les questions spéciales qui viendront à les réclamer et nommément sur les di verses réformes administratives, judiciaires et autres dont la Conférence, après en avoir posé le principe, a réservé l'accomplissement aux futures assemblées législatives d'accord ave le corps commun et avec les chefs de l'Etat.

APPENDIX II

GIERS' REPORT ON THE ELECTION OF CUZA IN WALLACHIA[2]

Ainsi que j'ai eu l'honneur de l'annoncer à Votre Excellence par ma dépêche télégraphique d'hier, l'Assemblée valaque vient d'élire à l'unanimité comme Hospodar Prince Alexandre Couza, élu à la même dignité il y a quelques semaines en Moldavie.

Pour expliquer les causes qui ont amené cet événement aussi important qu'inattendu je dois vous soumettre, mon Prince, le résumé des faits qui ont précédé l'élection. Je suivrai l'ordre des dates.

Le 22 de ce mois a eu lieu dans la salle de la Métropole l'ouverture solennelle de l'Assemblée en présence des hauts fonctionnaires de l'Etat et de tout le corps consulaire. Après la célébration du service divin la séance a été ouverte par un discours de la Caimacamie dont le Secrétaire d'Etat a donné lecture. J'ai l'honneur de placer sous les yeux de Votre Excellence le texte imprimé de cette allocution. Le Métropolitain, en sa qualité de président a déclaré ensuite que conformément aux dispositions du Règlement organique l'Assemblée était invitée à nommer la commission pour la vérification des pouvoirs des députés. Cette proposition a soulevé dès l'abord une discussion très vive. Le Beyzadé Demetre Ghika a demandé qu'avant de procéder à la vérification des pouvoirs l'Assemblée exclue de son sein les membres dont l'élection était entachée d'une illégalité notoire. Sur la refus du Métropolitain d'accéder à cette demande l'Ex-Hospodar Alexandre Ghika soutint la thèse posée par son neveu et après un discours passionné qui fut couvert par les applaudissements de la gauche et des tribunes il déclara que n'ayant pas été élu à la majorité absolue des suffrages, exigée par l'article 16 du Règlement électoral, il regardait son mandat de député comme nul et se retirait de la Chambre pour donner l'exemple de la légalité. Dès lors la discussion s'anima de plus en plus. Les esprits se passionnaient visiblement. Les accusations portées contre les illégalités de la Caimacamie devenaient irritantes et personnelles, les députés de la droite étaient à peine écoutés, le public dans les tribunes se livrait à des démonstrations tumultueuses. Après plusieurs heures de débats orageux auxquels Mr. Brattiano et consorts eurent la majeure part on convint enfin du principe de l'élimination préable des députés: 1., qui n'avaient pas réuni la majorité absolue des votes, 2., qui avaient été élus par acclamation et non au scrutin secret et 3., qui avaient été élus dans les collèges électoraux dont on avait exclu les électeurs reconnus pour tels par les sentences des tribunaux de 1$^{\underline{e}}$ instance. Neuf membres de l'Assemblée ayant été rangés dans ces trois catégories la séance fut levée.

Le soir du même jour plusieurs membres du parti conservateur vinrent me trouver pour me prier de continuer à assister aux séances de l'Assemblée qui sans la présence du corps consulaire ne tarderaient pas à donner lieu à des scènes de désordre et même de violence. Nous ne manquâmes pas, mes collègues et moi de nous rendre à cette invitation notre présence paraissant effectivement contribuer au maintien de l'ordre.

La séance du 23 fut plus orageuse encore que celle de la veille. Le Président ayant voulu procéder à la formation des commissions de vérification, les membres de la gauche s'y opposèrent demandant l'appel nominal afin que l'Assemblée pût statuer sur l'exclusion des députés qui en vertu du principe accepté la veille devaient à l'instar des 9 députés déjà désignés être éliminés des commissions. Cette proposition fut acceptée par la majorité et on s'occupait à passer en revue les titres des différents députés lorsque Mr. Jean Brattiano annonça à l'Assemblée l'arrivée dans la cour de la Métropole d'une compagnie de la milice en protestant vivement contre ce moyen d'intimidation. Cette nouvelle fut le signal d'un tumulte général dans la salle. Le public ne se contenait plus dans les tribunes et ses clameurs se joignaient aux cris de la populace au dehors dont le nombre allait toujours en croissant et qui menaçait de faire irruption dans la salle si la troupe n'était pas éloignée. Un instant la salle fut effectivement envahie par une 40e d'individus qui se retirèrent cependant quand ils apprirent qu'il serait fait droit à leur demande. Sous la pression de ces scènes il ne reste plus au Président qu'à inviter le Spatar à retirer la troupe mais en même temps à faire évacuer la cour de la Métropole par la populace. Cet ordre ne fut exécuté qu'à demi. Les soldats se retirèrent; la foule ne bougea pas. Cette satisfaction donnée, l'Assemblée reprit les délibérations mais sans pouvoir retrouver ni calme ni dignité. Les discussions se succédaient sans ordre aucun, les députés quittaient leurs places et s'adressaient des interpellations injurieuses, les tribunes se mêlaient aux débats et la sonnette du Président s'agitait en vain, couverte qu'elle était par les cris de la foule obéissant évidemment à des mots d'ordre qui lui arrivaient de la salle. La partie n'était plus égale; la majorité intimidée cédait sur tous les points. Le Métropolitain leva enfin la séance, mais conjuré par Mr. Brattiano il la reprit bientôt après, malgré l'absence d'une partie des députés. On s'efforça d'arriver à un résultat quelconque mais inutilement. La fatigue d'un côté, l'émotion de l'autre mirent enfin un terme à cette

léplorable séance, qui n'avait pas avancé d'un pas la discussion.
La formation des commissions fut remise au lendemain.

En attendant l'agitation gagnait la ville. Quelques scènes de
lésordre eurent lieu dans la soirée. Une patrouille de dorobantz
:ut désarmée par la foule et la maison de l'Ispravnik envahie. Un
3rand nombre de paysans accourus des environs grossissait les
attroupements formés par la population des faubourgs. Le
3ouvernement n'avait pas à sa disposition des moyens nécessaires
)our garantir la sécurité publique.

Frappés du danger que présentait cette situation tendue plusieurs députés prirent la résolution de provoquer le lendemain à
l'Assemblée une délibération secrète pour proposer d'exclure de
.a candidature à l'Hospodarat les trois ex-Princes et les chefs de
)arti exalté. Cette proposition qui offrait réellement un moyen
le calmer un peu les passions des partis opposés fut acceptée
aux débuts même de la séance d'hier. Tous les membres prirent part à la délibération secrète. On s'y était entendu sur les
exclusions proposées lorsqu'un des députés, Mr. Boyaresco,
)roposa dans un discours chaleureux de voter pour le Hospodar
le Moldavie. Cette décision fut suivie des démonstrations les
)lus enthousiastes. L'émotion avait gagné tout le monde et les
scènes de réconciliation succédaient aux accusations et aux in-
'ures.

Immédiatement après l'Assemblée a procédé à la formation
le quatre comités qui en peu de temps ont vérifié les pouvoirs,
)pération sur laquelle les deux jours précédents on n'avait pu
s'entendre. Six élections ont été annulées pour défaut de majorité.

Une fois constituée, l'Assemblée, composée de 64 membres,
/ compris le Métropolitain et les trois Evêques, a élu au scrutin
secret le Prince A. Couza. Des acclamations enthousiastes ont
accueilli la proclamation de ce vote unanime et des applaudissements ont éclaté en l'honneur des Puissances Suzeraine et ga-
rantes.

Toutes les formes prescrites en matière d'élection par le
Règlement organique et par la Convention ayant été scrupuleusement observées, la séance s'est prolongée jusqu'à 8 heures du
soir. Il est juste de dire également que l'Assemblée cette fois n'a
subi aucune pression au dehors car des dispositions avaient été
prises dès le matin pour empêcher la populace de pénétrer dans
.a cour de la Métropole. Ce n'est que lorsque l'élection du Prince
Couza fut proclamée que les abords de l'Assemblée furent ouverts
à la foule.

Le soir la ville était illuminée. L'inquiétude et les angoisses
le la veille ont fait place à une allégresse générale.

En soumettant à Votre Excellence ce simple exposé de faits
je m'abstiens pour le moment d'énoncer un jugement sur la portée
d'un événement que le Cabinet Impérial saura mieux apprécier

dans son enchaînement avec les intérêts de la politique générale en Europe.

APPENDIX III

A REPORT BY LOBANOV ON THE RUSSIAN POSITION IN CONSTANTINOPLE IN THE SUMMER OF 1859[3]

En accusant à Votre Excellence l'exacte réception de la lettre par laquelle Elle m'a fait l'honneur de me communiquer la dépêche de M. le Baron de Brunnow[4] de 6/18 juin, No. 190, je m'empresse de Lui offrir tous mes remerciements pour cette importante communication. Elle ne pouvait manquer de fixer ma plus sérieuse attention, et je dois ajouter, en ce qui regarde plus particulièrement les affaires de Turquie, que les remarquables aperçus de notre Ministre à Londres coïncident en tout point avec les observations que je suis moi-même dans le cas de faire journellement sur le terrain de Constantinople.

Quels que soient les changements qui surviennent dans le Ministère anglais ou dans l'Ambassade britannique à Constantinople, ces changements donnent seulement une impulsion plus ou moins prononcée à la politique anglaise en Orient, mais, au fond, les principes qui les dirigent restent toujours les mêmes: c'est une défiance profonde à l'égard de la Russie, que l'Angleterre considère comme sa seule rivale sérieuse en Orient, et, comme conséquence de ce sentiment, la résolution de maintenir à tout prix l'intégrité de l'Empire Ottoman.

Pour l'Angleterre, toutes les autres considérations méritent à peine d'attirer son attention. Au lieu d'envisager le développement et les tendances des nationalités chrétiennes de la Turquie d'un point de vue élevé et seul digne d'une Puissance civilisée, elle n'y voit qu'un accroissement de l'influence russe dans l'avenir.

Il est inadmissible que les hommes d'état anglais croient à la durée indéfinie de l'Empire Ottoman; les garanties inscrites en faveur de l'intégrité territoriale de la Turquie, d'abord dans le préambule du protocole de Londres de 1841, et ensuite dans le texte des deux traités du 30 mars et du 15 avril 1856, sont là pour attester le peu de confiance que l'on a généralement dans la durée de cet état de choses. Mais, à mesure que ces appréhensions deviennent plus sérieuses, l'Angleterre semble mettre une persévérance plus opiniâtre à profiter de chaque occasion pour essayer de consolider l'autorité turque non seulement dans les provinces qui en dépendent directement, mais aussi dans les pays qui sont simplement sous la suzeraineté de la Porte, et malgré

les fréquents démentis que lui donne la marche logique et irré-
sistible des événements, elle continue à proclamer, par l'organe
de ses représentants, qu'elle est résolue de ne permettre aucune
altération dans ce qui existe actuellement en Turquie.

En dehors de cet intérêt politique général, l'Angleterre ne
semble avoir en Turquie aucun intérêt particulier. Ce désintéressement apparent donne au rôle de l'Angleterre une grande sim-
plicité d'action et a contribué àu lui créer auprès du Governemen
turc une position prépondérante, qui, jusqu'à la conclusion de la
paix de 1856, n'avait pas de rivale. Si, depuis cette époque, l'influence anglaise a baissé à Constantinople, c'est que l'expérience
des dernières années a démontré à la Porte d'une manière écla-
tante qu'après tout, la volonté de l'Angleterre n'était pas toute
puissante en Europe et qu'elle n'avait pu empêcher ni un achemine
ment vers l'union des Principautés moldo-valaques, ni une quasi-
reconnaissance de l'indépendance du Monténégro, — deux question
pour lesquelles Lord Palmerston, au point de vue anglais, a une
répugnance parfaitement justifiée.

Par une déduction toute naturelle, ce qui fait la force de l'An
gleterre auprès du Gouvernement turc, fait sa faiblesse auprès
des populations chrétiennes; elle n'a sur celles-ci aucune influenc
et s'est toujours montrée fort peu soucieuse d'en acquérir.

De même que l'Angleterre, l'Autriche attache une importance
majeure à la conservation de ce qui existe en Turquie; c'est mêm
pour elle un intérêt vital, une condition sine qua non de sa propre
sécurité. Composée comme elle est d'une agglomération hétéro-
gène de diverses nationalités, dont quelques-unes sont les mêmes
qu'en Turquie, elle redoute à chaque changement qui s'opère chez
sa voisine ou qui menace de s'y opérer, un contrecoup dans ses
propres provinces limitrophes. Le Baron de Prokesch m'a ré-
pété plus d'une fois qu'une entente entre la Russie et l'Autriche
était désirable et même nécessaire pour le maintien de la paix
générale, et que cette entente pouvait s'étendre facilement à toute
les questions européennes; mais que, pour ce qui concerne les
questions d'Orient, une entente entre les deux Gouvernments
n'était possible qu'autant que nous nous rencontrerions avec l'Autriche sur le terrain du maintien absolu de l'intégrité géographique
de la Turquie et de la consolidation de l'autorité de la Porte dans
ses différentes possessions. Selon lui, le Prince Metternich aurait franchement et nettement exposé cette idée dans le Congrès
de Münchengrätz, à l'époque de la plus grande intimité entre les
deux Cours Impériales, et depuis lors elle est demeurée comme
un principe invariable de la politique autrichienne.

Il est vrai, cette communauté d'intérêts entre l'Autriche et la
Turquie, quelque réelle qu'elle soit, n'a jamais pu faire croire à
Constantinople au désintéressement complet du Cabinet de Vienne
comme cela est le cas pour celui de Londres. Bien que l'Autrich
soit essentiellement une Puissance qui doive chercher plutôt à

conserver ce qu'elle possède, qu'à faire de nouvelles acquisitions, cependant, à tort ou à raison, elle a toujours été soupçonnée de convoiter quelque chose en Turquie, —soit les Principautés danubiennes, soit la Bosnie. La propagande politique et religieuse qu'elle fait dans cette dernière province, ainsi qu'en Albanie, la protection qu'elle veut y exercer sur le culte catholique à l'exclusion de la France, avec laquelle elle se trouve sous ce rapport en constante rivalité, peuvent jusqu'à un certain point justifier ces soupçons et entretenir la méfiance que les allures traditionnelles du Cabinet de Vienne sont en général de nature à inspirer.

Néanmoins, il ne faut pas se dissimuler que l'action combinée de l'Angleterre et de l'Autriche a un point d'appui très solide à Constantinople, et qu'elle peut nous y susciter de grands embarras, malgré le rétablissement de relations plus amicales entre la Russie et la Porte. Mais, dans cette hypothèse, il est plus que probable que l'expérience de ces dernières années ne restera pas perdue pour ces deux Puissances, et qu'elles mettront tout en oeuvre pour attirer la France de leur côté. Je ne crois pas me tromper en affirmant que telle est en effet l'idée intime de l'Ambassadeur d'Angleterre à Constantinople. L'Internonce d'Autriche, de son côté, a subitement changé de language depuis la conclusion de la paix avec la France; il ne tarit pas d'éloges sur la modération et la loyauté de l'Empereur Napoléon, et met beaucoup d'affection à proclamer que désormais les rapports entre l'Autriche et la France viennent d'entrer dans une période toute nouvelle.

Jusqu'à présent rien n'indique dans les relations de la France et de la Russie que l'entente qui s'est établie, entre elles relativement aux affaires d'Orient, doive cesser prochainement. Mais, afin d'en apprécier les chances de durée, il est permis de se demander si de la part de la France elle repose réellement sur quelque intérêt permanent, sur une politique persévérante qui n'aurait jamais dévié de son but et qui concorderait entièrement avec la nôtre.[5]

Il me semble que poser cette question, c'est la résoudre. L'action de la France en Orient a toujours été si variable, qu'il est difficile de démêler le principe qui en est le point de départ. Tel que je l'ai entendu développer par M. Thouvenel, il consisterait à prêter à la Porte un concours loyal pour soutenir et consolider l'autorité du Sultan dans toute l'étendue de ses Etats, tout en favorisant le développement du bien-être et de la prospérité des populations chrétiennes. Assurément, c'est là un principe qui, en apparence, est de nature à satisfaire tout le monde, et ceux qui tiennent par-dessus tout, à soutenir et à étendre l'autorité de la Porte, comme ceux qui ont à coeur de voir cesser un jour les souffrances des populations chrétiennes et de préparer graduellement leur émancipation à venir. Mais dans son application pratique, ce principe ne saurait tracer une ligne de conduite toujours la même, car il contient deux idées qui s'excluent réciproquement et que l'on ne peut vouloir concilier sans tomber dans de fréquentes contradictions avec soi-même. La politique de la France le démontre suffisamment. Elle a toujours procédé en Orient sans suite, presque au hasard, en s'inspirant alternativement soit d'une crainte exagérée à l'égard de projets ambitieux attribués à la Russie, soit des tendances libérales que tout Gouvernement en France, quel qu'il soit, cherche à faire prévaloir à l'extérieur. C'est ainsi qu'immédiatement après la guerre d'Orient, les préventions contre nous ayant fait place à des relations d'une intime confiance entre les deux Gouvernements, on a vu la France se faire le champion des aspirations nationales dans les Principautés moldo-valaques et adopter, à l'égard du Monténégro, la politique séculaire de la Russie. En revanche, la Servie, qui certes a un droit égal à la protection du monde civilisé, reste frustrée de la bienveillance du Gouvernement français. Cette contradiction serait inexplicable, si elle ne laissait entrevoir de la part du Gouvernement français, malgré nos relations intimes avec lui, l'arrière-pensée de substituer son influence exclusive à celle que nous avons exercée dans ces différentes contrées; la tiédeur, pour ne pas dire le mauvais vouloir de la France envers la Servie provient de ce que la grande majorité du peuple y continue à professer hautement une reconnaissance et un dévouement traditionnel pour la Russie et que le Prince Milosch,[6] malgré sa sauvage rudesse, témoigne beaucoup plus de déférence envers nos conseils qu'envers ceux des autres Puissances, —tandis que le Prince Daniel[7] et les patriotes roumains ont accepté le patronage de la France avec une soumission empressée.

Il est inutile de faire remarquer qu'une politique aussi peu conséquente avec elle-même n'a jamais été capable d'assurer à la France un crédit durable à Constantinople. Il n'a toujours dépendu que de la signification de la France dans les affaires générales de l'Europe, sans que le Gouvernement français ait jamais pu inspirer une entière confiance à la Porte. Cette vérité est ressortie d'une manière particulièrement frappante pendant la dernière guerre d'Orient et dans les premiers temps qui suivirent la conclusion de la paix l'influence des deux Puissances occidentales à Constantinople était à cette époque en proportion inverse des sacrifices de chacune d'elles pour la défense de la Turquie.

Le seul intérêt que la France ait poursuivi en Orient avec quelque persévérance, c'est celui que lui impose sa qualité de Puissance catholique. A ce titre, elle exerce, par une ancienne tradition, une protection exclusive sur le rite latin en Orient. Les contestations et l'antagonisme religieux entre les Orthodoxes et les Catholiques ont fait l'objet d'une entente spéciale entre la Russie et la France, et, grâce à cette prévoyante disposition, on ne voit pas se produire au grand jour entre les agents des deux Puissances des rivalités regrettables qui auraient pu influer sur les relations des deux Gouvernements. Mais une guerre sourde

continue avec le même acharnement que par le passé. Sans par-
ler de la Syrie, où la lutte entre les deux rites n'a jamais cessé,
il suffit de connaître la propagande active qui se fait dans la Turquie d'Europe, et nommément en Bulgarie: des missionnaires
catholiques, pour la plupart des Lazaristes, dont l'établissement
central est à Constantinople sous la protection de la France, par-
courent toute la Bulgarie et y prêchent l'union avec Rome, en
tâchant d'exciter partout la désaffection pour la Russie et en pro-
mettant une protection énergique de la part de la France.

On peut conclure de ce qui précède que l'entente entre la
France et la Russie repose en Orient sur une base très fragile.
Pour être dans le vrai, il faut dire qu'elle est la conséquence d'un
besoin réciproque que chacune d'elles éprouve, de pouvoir compter sur le concours de l'autre, —la Russie, pour ne pas se trouver dans l'isolement à Constantinople, et la France, pour se prévaloir de l'appui moral de la Russie dans les affaires de l'Europe.

Mais, dans l'état d'incertitude et de continuelle perturbation
que traverse maintenant l'Europe, nul ne peut prévoir ce que ren-
ferme dans son sein l'avenir le plus rapproché, et je n'aperçois
en Orient aucun motif grave qui puisse empêcher un accord inattendu entre la France et l'Angleterre dans les affaires de la Turquie. On a beaucoup exagéré l'antagonisme des deux Puissances
occidentales, en le jugeant d'après les rivalités toutes personelles
qui se sont manifestées entre leurs représentants respectifs à
Constantinople. Tout au plus peut-on dire qu'il existe en Egypte à
l'occasion du percement de l'Isthme de Suez. Mais là encore il
faut observer que jusqu'à présent le Gouvernement français a évi-
té avec le plus grand soin de protéger officieusement l'entreprise
de M. de Lesseps. D'ailleurs l'opinion publique en Angleterre
paraît être tellement partagée sur cette question, qu'au besoin le
Gouvernement anglais pourrait sans inconvénients, faire le sacrifice de son opposition à cette entreprise, si cela devenait nécessaire pour le rétablissement d'une action commune avec la
France.

En soumettant ces observations à l'indulgente appréciation de
Votre Excellence, je crois presque superflu d'ajouter que je suis
trop pénétré de la nécessité pour nous de maintenir un complet
accord avec la France, pour ne pas employer tous mes soins à
consolider les relations de confiance qui existent déjà depuis trois
ans entre la Légation Impériale et l'Ambassade de France et à
remplir ainsi, aussi scrupuleusement que possible, les hautes intentions du Cabinet Impérial. Nous avons en notre faveur des an-
técédents qui servent de lien entre la France et nous: ce sont
ceux des questions orientales, où elle a déjà pris une attitude,
qui ne semble plus lui permettre de reculer.

J'ose vous prier, Mon Prince, de vouloir bien excuser la
longueur des développements dans lesquels j'ai cru devoir entrer.
Ils m'ont paru nécessaires pour tracer avec une certaine

précision la position des différentes Puissances dans les affaires
de la Turquie.

APPENDIX IV

EXTRACTS FROM THE LETTERS OF LOBANOV TO GIERS
ON THE LEGISLATIVE AND ADMINISTRATIVE UNION
OF THE PRINCIPALITIES

1. Pera, January 31/February 12, 1861.

   Votre dernier télégramme m'a ébouriffé. Vous devez avoir été tout aussi surpris que moi de cette prétendue autorisation que la Porte aurait donnée à Couza de consommer l'Union, et je suis fort impatient de connaître ce qui a donné lieu à ce quiproquo. Il est vrai, la Porte n'envisage plus l'Union avec le même parti pris de résistance, mais il y a encore loin de là à accorder à Couza un droit qu'elle n'a pas elle-même et qu'elle ne pourrait conférer que du consentement de toutes les Puissances signataires de la Convention. Depuis que Négry nous a remis son mémoire, j'ai à plusieurs reprises interpellé la Porte sur son opinion; tout récemment votre télégramme m'a fourni une nouvelle occasion pour revenir à la charge: la réponse invariable d'Aali Pasha a été que la Porte n'avait pas encore fixé ses idées à cet égard, et qu'elle serait même bien aise de connaître d'avance les opinions des autres Puissances afin de ne pas s'exposer à émettre un avis isolé contraire à celui des Cabinets. Or jusqu'à présent, ceux-ci ne se sont pas encore prononcés. Pour notre part, le Prince Gortchacow m'a écrit qu'il en avait fait l'objet d'une entente avec les autres Cabinets et qu'il m'informerait du résultat.

   * * *

2. Pera, February 13/25, 1861.

   L'Union continue à faire l'objet de différentes conversations entre la Porte et les représentants. Vous connaissez par ma dépêche No. 189 l'opinion de Lavalette;[8] il y ajoute seulement, comme correctif, que l'on pourrait accorder à Couza à <u>titre viager</u>, l'autorisation de consommer l'Union. Bulwer, à ma grande surprise, est devenu très ardent pour la même question.

   Dernièrement nous nous sommes trouvés par hasard, sans aucune préméditation, réunis au coin du feu chez Lavalette; il y avait Bulwer, Goltz[9] et moi. La conversation est tout naturellement tombée sur la Moldo-Valachie. Lavalette et Bulwer se sont mis à développer l'idée suivante: "le malaise et l'agitation des Principautés proviennent de ce que Couza n'a pas tenu ce qu'on attendait de lui; l'opposition en profite pour lui reprocher constamment de n'avoir pas fait l'Union; en y autorisant Couza, les Puissances fortifieraient sa position en même temps qu'elle préviendraient l'explosion de troubles graves."

J'ai répondu que n'ayant pas encore d'instructions de mon Gouvernement, je ne pouvais qu'exprimer une opinion personnelle.

Pour ma part, ai-je dit, je n'ai ni sympathie ni antipathie pour l'Union; mais, avant de conseiller ce remède au malaise des Principautés, il est bon d'en examiner les conséquences probables. Que reproche l'opposition de Couza? De n'avoir pas rempli le programme des Unionistes? Mais, lorsqu'il aura consommé l'Union, ce programme sera-t-il rempli? Evidemment non, car ce programme, c'est Union avec le <u>Prince étranger</u>. La double élection de Couza ne devait être aux yeux des Unionistes qu'une transition; le jour où l'Union sera consommée on ne voudra plus de Couza: on demandera le Prince étranger.

A ces mots, Bulwer se récria que c'était une énormité à laquelle ni la Porte ni les Puissances ne consentiraient jamais.

Pas autant que vous le pensez, ai-je répliqué. La double élection de Couza était aussi une énormité dans son temps, et pourtant on l'a sanctionnée. On a dit formellement alors qu'à l'exception de cette déviation unique, la Convention serait maintenue dans son intégrité, —et nous voilà discutant sérieusement s'il y a lieu ou non de consommer l'Union. Une fois engagés dans ces systèmes de déviations partielles et successives, nous en arriverons de même à discuter la question du Prince étranger, —et, moins il restera pour l'accomplissement du programme unioniste, plus il sera difficile et même illogique de s'y opposer. Ajoutez-y que maintenant c'est Couza qui demande l'Union, dans le vain espoir de reconquérir sa popularité; alors ce sera tout le pays qui ne voudra plus de Couza, et qui demandera le Prince étranger, car, d'après ce que m'écrit M. de Giers, personne ne veut voir le pouvoir concentré entre les mains de Couza et de ses acolytes; cette considération est même, à ce qu'il paraît, assez puissante pour avoir fait perdre beaucoup de terrain à l'idée de l'Union.

La conclusion de ce que je viens de dire est celle-ci: si les Puissances s'accordent pour déférer au voeu de Couza, elle doivent dès à présent s'attendre à toutes les conséquences de leur résolution, et nommément à être mises prochainement en demeure de sanctionner l'élection d'un Prince étranger; or, le Prince étranger c'est l'indépendance complète de la Moldo-Valachie, attendu qu'aucun membre d'une Maison Souveraine de l'Europe ne se soumettra à la suzeraineté de la Porte.

Ce résultat, ai-je ajouté en riant, pourrait ne pas me répugner mais il ne s'agit pas de cela, et je ne fais que signaler sans détour ce qui, à nos yeux, serait la conséquence inévitable de l'Union.

Pendant ce speech je me suis procuré le malin plaisir d'observer la contenance de chacun des mes interlocuteurs. Goltz paraissait très satisfait, et me l'a même dit plus tard. Bulwer

n'a rien répondu cependant mes paroles ne semblaient pas lui
déplaire; son ardeur Unioniste est toute factice, Lavalette était
sans contredit très désappointé; on aurait dit que je venais de
déchirer un voile qui couvrait les arrière-pensées de son Gouvernement. Pour dissimuler son embarras, il fit observer que,
dans l'état actuel de la question, il s'agissait simplement de savoir
s'il fallait conseiller à la Porte une résistance absolue aux deman-
des de Couza, ou bien s'il ne serait pas plus sage de l'engager à
les examiner d'accord avec les autres Puissances, en tenant
compte des difficultés de la situation. Je ne pus m'empêcher de
faire remarquer à Lavalette que c'était là une question tout-à-fait
secondaire, et que, pour ma part, je venais d'exprimer une opinion, à la vérité, toute personelle, sur le fond même de la
question, et non pas sur le plus ou moins de convenance qu'il y
aurait à la faire entrer dans le domaine des délibérations officiel-
les des Gouvernements. Cette conversation en resta là, et,
après quelques instants de silence, on parla d'autre chose.

Je ne vous ai rien dit des opinions de Prokesch, parce qu'elles sont faciles à deviner. Il dit qu'il y a sous la domination
autrichienne environ 3 millions de Roumains; si l'Union s'accom-
plissait, ils tendraient nécessairement à s'unir à leurs compatrio-
tes de Moldavie et de Valachie; c'est donc pour l'Autriche une
condition de son intégrité de s'opposer de la manière la plus absolue à l'Union des deux Principautés.

J'attends avec impatience que notre Cabinet m'ait fait part de
son appréciation.

* * *

3. Pera, February 27/March 11, 1861.

Je vois par votre lettre du 14 février que nous nous sommes
presque rencontrés avec vous dans notre appréciation de la
question de l'Union. Dans mes conversations avec mes collègues,
ainsi que dans ma correspondance avec le Ministère, j'ai posé la
question du Prince étranger comme étant intimement liée à celle
de la consommation de l'Union. J'ai la conviction que, dans l'opinion même du pays, l'une entraînera nécessairement l'autre.
Reste à savoir si cette impulsion sera conforme à nos intérêts.
Quel serait ce Prince étranger, couvert actuellement du voile de
l'inconnu? Je pense que personne ne saurait le dire; la seule
chose qui me paraisse certaine, c'est que, quel qu'il soit, il n'aura
plus les hésitations de Couza et entrera résolument dans la voie
où celui-ci ne s'engage qu'en tâtonnant. De toute nécessité il ne
sera pas orthodoxe, car ce n'est pas chez nous qu'on ira le chercher; il sera catholique, et consommera l'oeuvre de la latinisation
du pays; avec elle, il arborera le drapeau des sympathies romai-
nes, italiennes, révolutionnaires, etc, —et pourra compter plus
encore que Couza sur l'appui de la France. Je reconnais que ces
tendances existent déjà dans les Principautés, et, comme dit le

proverbe, suzhenago konem ne ob'edesh',[10] mais que gagnerions nous à un changement de ce genre, si ce n'est de hâter une situation qui dans ce moment serait pour nous un grave embarras. Reculer le terme de quelques années, tel doit être, ce me semble, le but de nos efforts, et, pour ma part, je n'hésite pas à me prononcer pour l'ajournement de la question de l'union.

* * *

4. Buyukdere, August 14/26, 1861.

... je vous envoie ci-joint deux dépêches que j'adresse en cour dont l'une ne partira que demain. Elle rendent compte de nos conversations avec le Chargé d'affaires de France. Son Gouvernment ne paraît guère tenir compte des idées développées par notre Cabinet et persiste dans son idée sur l'urgence de l'Union. Comme le point de vue exprimé dans le télégramme de Thouvenel est complètement différent du nôtre, j'ai dû en référer à Pétersburg, ne sachant pas si, depuis les dernières dépêches que j'ai reçues du Prince Gortchacow, il n'y a pas eu quelques nouvelles communications échangées entre les 2 Cabinets. Quant à présent, ce que je vois c'est que nous ne sommes pas parvenus à faire partager nos opinions au Gouvernement français et que l'entente, si souvent désirée par nous, n'existe pas encore sur ce point, qui pourtant est très important au point de vue de nos intérêts.

* * *

5. Buyukdere, October 9/21, 1861.

... je n'ai rien à vous annoncer aujourd'hui. Vous aurez reçu directement de Pétersburg la dépêche que le Prince Gortchacow m'a adressée en date du 19 septembre; elle est très claire et très explicite. Aali Pasha auquel je l'ai communiquée, m'a dit que la Porte, après les vacances de Hospodarat, ne se refuserait pas à examiner, selon les voeux qu'exprimeraient les Moldo-Valaques, s'il y a lieu ou non de continuer l'Union, et qu'elle n'avait pas l'intention d'employer dans ce cas les mesures coercitives. Il a ajouté, qu'il voyait bien qu'on avait tendu un piège à la Porte, en l'assurant que l'Union ne devrait être que viagère, —et que de toutes les Puissances la Russie était la seule qui eût toujours tenu un langage franc et loyal. Il attribue la politique qui guide certaines Puissances dans cette affaire au désir d'établir sur les bords du Danube un foyer révolutionnaire qui peut, au besoin, être employé utilement comme arme de guerre contre l'une des Puissances limitrophes. Je pense qu'il n'a que trop raison.

* * *

6. Pera, January 1/13, 1863.

Je vous remercie infiniment pour votre dernière expédition. Elle ne fait que confirmer mes opinions en ce qui regarde les résultats de l'Union. La Porte finira par se mordre les doigts d'avoir trop facilement cédé aux suggestions françaises. Reste à savoir si, malgré ses pompeuses proclamations, Couza y trouvera personnellement un élément de force et de stabilité.

*   *   *

Notes

1. Giers to Popov, No. 14, Bucharest, October 10/22, 1858.

2. Giers to Gorchakov, No. 8, Bucharest, January 25/February 6, 1859.

3. Copy of a despatch from Lobanov to Gorchakov, No. 96, very confidential, (Buyukdere), July 18/30, 1859.

4. Filipp Ivanovich Brunov. The Russian ambassador in London.

5. Throughout Lobanov's letters to Giers an undercurrent of disapprobation of Gorchakov's policy of friendship with France exists. Lobanov appears to have objected not so much to French policy as such, but to the fact that in so many matters Russia followed France. He certainly did not look with favor on the events in Italy. On July 20/August 1 he wrote:

> Où va l'Europe? C'est la question que chacun est en droit de s'adresser. D'après les communications que j'ai reçues aujourd'hui de Pétersburg, il paraît que la conclusion d'une paix dans laquelle on a l'air de se moquer de l'opinion de l'Europe pour annuler, sans son consentement, les derniers vestiges des traités de 1815, a vivement surpris et blessé à Pétersburg. Je vois l'avenir très en noir; l'équilibre européen n'existe plus; nous sommes dans le chaos, sans que personne ait encore pris son assiette politique et sache où sont les amis et les ennemis. Il n'y a aucune garantie pour la paix générale, à moins qu'on ne rétablisse quelque chose de semblable à ce qui a assuré cette paix pendant une durée de quarante années. Mais ceci n'est plus mon affaire ...

Lobanov to Giers, private letter, Buyukdere, July 20/August 1, 1859.

Later Lobanov wrote in approval:

> Nos rapports avec la France sont aussi intimes que par le passé, mais notre politique ne semble plus aussi exclusive, et, au lieu de tenir regards fixés uniquement sur Paris, nous regardons aussi à droite et à gauche, à Berlin comme à Vienne ... Petit à petit nous reprenons tout l'ascendant de notre ancienne position.

Lobanov to Giers, private letter, Pera, October 26/November 7, 1859.

6. Miloš Obrenović. The ruler of Serbia at this time.

7. Danilo. The prince of Montenegro.

8. Charles Félix Lavalette. The French ambassador at Constantinople.

9. Karl von der Goltz. The Prussian minister at Constantinople.

10. (translation) You cannot escape your fate.

BIBLIOGRAPHY

(Confined to works cited in the previous pages)

PUBLISHED DOCUMENTS, MEMOIRS, CORRESPONDENCE, ETC.

Bengesco, Grégoire, Memorandum sur les églises, les monastères, les biens conventuels et spécialement sur les monastères dédiés de la Principauté de Valachie, (Bucharest:
Imprimerie C. A. Rosetti, 1858).

Bismarck, Otto von, Die gesammelten Werke, edited by H. von
Petersdorff, (Berlin: Stollberg, 1925), III.

Bossy, R. V., Agenția diplomaticǎ a României în Paris, (Bucharest: Cartea Romȃneascǎ, 1931).

Bossy, R. V., L'Autriche et les Principautés-Unies, (Bucharest:
Imprimerie nationale, 1938).

Fotino, George, Din vremea renaşterii naţionale a Țǎrii Romȃ-
neşti—Boierii Goleşti, (Bucharest: Imprimeria naţionalǎ,
1939), IV.

France. Ministère des affaires étrangères, Documents diplomatiques. 1861, (Paris: Imprimerie impériale, 1862).

Friese, Christian, editor, Die auswärtige Politik Preussens, 1858
1871, (Oldenburg: Gerhard Stalling, 1933-1945), I, II, II^2.

Henry, Paul, L'Abdication du Prince Cuza et l'avènement de la
dynastie de Hohenzollern au trône de Roumanie, (Paris: Librairie Félix Alcan, 1930).

Hoetzsch, Otto, editor, Peter von Meyendorff: Ein russischer Diplomat an den Höfen von Berlin und Wien, (Berlin and Leipzig:
Walter de Gruyter, 1923), III.

Hübner, Count Joseph Alexander von, Neuf ans de souvenirs d'un
ambassadeur d'Autriche sous le Second Empire, (Paris: Librairie Plon, 1904), II.

Nesselrode, Comte A. de, editor, Lettres et papiers du chancellier
Comte de Nesselrode, 1760-1856, (Paris: A. Lahure, n.d.),
XI.

Reinach, S., "Charles Tissot à Jassy (et à la Commission des
Couvents dédiés); 1863-1866," Revue historique du Sud-Est
européen, I, Nos. 7-9, 1924, pp. 205-233.

Schlözer, Kurd von, Petersburger Briefe, 1857-1862, (Stuttgart and Berlin: Deutsche Verlags-Anstalt, 1922).

Sturdza, D. A., editor, Acte și Documente relative la Istoria Renascerei României, (Bucharest: Carol Göbl, 1900-1909), I-X.

Thouvenel, L., Trois années de la question d'orient, 1856-1859, (Paris: Calmann Lévy, 1897).

GENERAL WORKS

Berindei, Dan, "Frămîntările grănicerilor și dorobanților în jurul formării taberei de la Florești (vara anului 1859)," Academia Republicii Populare Romîne, Studii: Revistă de istorie, X, nr. 3, 1957, pp. 113-133.

Berindei, Dan, "Frămîntări politice și sociale în jurul alegerii domnitorului Cuza în Țara Romînească," Academia Republicii Populare Romîne, Studii: Revistă de istorie, VIII, nr. 2, 1955, pp. 51-74.

Campbell, John C., French Influence and the Rise of Roumanian Nationalism: The Generation of 1848: 1830-1857, (unpublished thesis, Harvard, 1940).

Charles-Roux, François, Alexandre II, Gortchakoff et Napoléon III, (Paris: Librairie Plon, 1913).

Damé, Frédéric, Histoire de la Roumanie contemporaine, (Paris: Félix Alcan, 1900).

East, W. G., The Union of Moldavia and Wallachia, 1859, (Cambridge: University Press, 1929).

Emerit, M., Les paysans roumains depuis le traité d'Andrinople jusqu'à la libération des terres, (Paris: Librairie du Recueil Sirey, 1937).

Evans, Ifor L., The Agrarian Revolution in Roumania, (Cambridge: University Press, 1924).

Filitti, Jean C., Les Principautés roumaines sous l'occupation russe, 1828-1834, (Bucharest: Imprimerie de l'"Indépendence Roumaine," 1904).

Friese, Christian, Russland und Preussen vom Krimkrieg bis zum Polnischen Aufstand, (Berlin: Ost-Europa Verlag, 1931).

Hallberg, Charles W., Franz Joseph and Napoleon III, 1852-1864, (New York: Bookman Associates, 1955).

Iorga, N., Geschichte des Rumänischen Volkes in Rahmen seiner Staatsbildungen, (Gotha: Friedrich Andreas Perthes, 1905).

Iorga, N., Histoire des relations russo-roumaines, (Jassy: Edition du journal "Neamul Romănesc," 1917).

Iorga, N., Histoire des Roumaines et de la Romanite Orientale (Bucharest: Académie roumaine, 1944), IX.

Mitrany, David, The Land and the Peasant in Rumania, (London: Oxford University Press, 1930).

Nolde, Boris, Die Petersburger Mission Bismarcks, 1859-1862, (Leipzig: Verlag Rudolf Lamm, 1936).

Petrovich, Michael Boro, The Emergence of Russian Panslavism, 1856-1870, (New York: Columbia University Press, 1956).

Politics and Political Parties in Roumania, (London: International Reference Library Publishing Company, 1936).

Riasanovsky, Nicholas V., Nicholas I and Official Nationality in Russia, 1825-1855, (Berkeley: University of California Press 1959).

Riker, T. W., The Making of Roumania, (Oxford: Oxford University Press, 1931).

Roberts, Henry L., Rumania: Political Problems of an Agrarian State, (New Haven: Yale University Press, 1951).

Schüle, Ernst, Russland und Frankreich vom Ausgang des Krimkrieges bis zum italienischen Krieg, 1856-1859, (Königsberg and Berlin: Ost-Europa-Verlag, 1935).

Seton-Watson, R. W., A History of the Roumanians, (Cambridge: University Press, 1934).

Sumner, B. H., Russia and the Balkans, 1870-1880, (Oxford: Clarendon Press, 1937).

Sumner, B. H., "The Secret Franco-Russian Treaty of 3 March 1859," English Historical Review, XLVIII, 1933, pp. 65-83.

Xénopol, A. D., Histoire des Roumains de la Dacie trajane depuis les origines jusqu'à l'union des Principautés en 1859, (Paris: Ernest Leroux, 1896), II.

Xenopol, A. D., Istoria Românilor din Dacia Traiană, (Bucharest: Cartea Românească, n.d.), XIII, XIV.

Zablotskii-Desiatovskii, A. P., Graf P. D. Kiselev i ego Vremia, (St. Petersburg: M. M. Stasiulevich, 1882), III.

INDEX